ENDURE

The Power of
Spiritual Assets
for Resilience to
Trauma & Stress

DANIEL D. MAURER

Endure: The Power of Spiritual Assets for Resilience to Trauma & Stress by Daniel D. Maurer

Copyright © 2017 by Mount Curve Press.

Printed in the United States of America

First Printing 2017

Paperback
ISBN 10: 0-9973286-0-6
ISBN 13: 978-0-9973286-0-8

Ebook
ISBN 10: 0-9973286-1-4
ISBN 13: 978-0-9973286-1-5

For Cathy, Hunter, Kitty, Raja, Jennifer, and Rick. Resilience is real and so is transformation.

Also, for my wife Carol, without whose steadfast belief in my ability to endure would have made my journey much lonelier.

Introduction

It was a cold afternoon in January when I was arrested. I was lying in bed. I had just woken up from a nap, that sweet bliss of non-existence, a grave I'd dig myself into, usually interrupted only by the occasional dream. Only by that time in my life, I had quit dreaming much, either in my sleep or awake. I was lost and my dreams were too.

My wife, Carol, walked into the bedroom. She had come home from work early.

She said, "Get up. The Sheriff's department is here to arrest you."

That sinking feeling, the one that had been with me that whole year, solidified and dropped to the pit of my gut. I got up, pulled on a pair of jeans and walked downstairs where the deputies slapped a pair of handcuffs on me.

"Do you really have to do that?" Carol asked.

"Yes. It's procedure," the female deputy answered.

I recognized her. She was the Williams County detective who had grilled me over that past month in a windowless room with two cheap, plastic chairs and a little card table in the government building in Williston, North Dakota, the proverbial "heart" of the oil boom going full bore in western North Dakota. I remembered thinking why the hell the department couldn't afford better furniture, with all the oil money people were tossing around. Evidently, the authorities don't care whether a suspect is comfortable when they question them.

I wasn't very comfortable, come to think of it. Not at all. The steel handcuffs bit into my wrists. A male deputy rattled off my Miranda rights.

"Do you understand these rights as I've explained them?"

"Huh?" I replied.

"I'm telling you what you need to know, Mr. Maurer. Do you understand?" he asked. He sounded impatient.

"Yeah. I guess."

The deputies guided me to the SUV idling just outside my home. There was a big star printed on the vehicle's door. The chill Dakota air bit my face as I walked. The events seemed surreal. I remember the back seat of the Sheriff's vehicle was comfortably warm. I looked into the front at the driver, another deputy, and I said, "Hi."

He didn't respond.

I can't remember whether the detective told me what I had been arrested for when they were handcuffing me. By that time in my life, my mind wasn't working too well, so it doesn't surprise me that I can't recall everything. I do remember, though, that I wanted to know what the official charges were. I had an inkling what was going on; I just wanted them to tell me. I somehow recalled a fact from a high school social studies course, that people have a right to know who their accusers are. The female detective opened the passenger door of the SUV and got in.

"I have a right to know who my accusers are and what I'm being charged for," I said, with a splash of arrogance and indignation, somehow to let her know that I was important, that I was *somebody.*

She paused. Then she took out a brown clipboard, turned to a page with an official document, and showed it to me. She pointed to the top of the page and said, "We're arresting you for felony trespass."

It wasn't the first time I had been arrested. However, the first time I barely remembered anything. I do know that I had woken up sick with the shakes, and it must have been before one in the morning because I knew the liquor stores closed at that time. If they hadn't been open, I wouldn't have gone out. Instead, I had stumbled to my black F-150 pickup and drove to the store to renew my stash and stop the shakes so I could get back to sleep. I guess when I was backing out of the liquor store parking lot to return home, I turned the steering wheel too quickly and I drove my pickup into another vehicle's mirror and smashed it. I'm sure it was either the vehicle's owner or the store attendant who called the cops on me. Of course, it didn't really matter, because on the way back to my house, I ended up sliding off the icy road and into a ditch. When I got out of my pickup, the cops were already there.

One thing I do remember about the incident is that I told the cops I had a tow chain in the bed of my pickup. This makes me laugh—I was so damned drunk that I didn't know that the police were there to arrest me, not lend a hand pulling me out of the ditch with the handy chain I kept in the back.

Really, that first arrest wasn't so bad. In a stupor and the relative comfort of the blur of drunkenness, time goes by more quickly. Most of that time in the hard, cold cell, I was asleep. I blacked out.

The second time wasn't as easy. Not by a long shot.

I was going through withdrawal from both alcohol and benzos.

By that time, my substance usage bounced between mostly alcohol and pills—benzodiazepines, preferably Xanax, or painkillers when I could get them. Benzodiazepines are a class of medication that doctors prescribe for patients who suffer from anxiety, panic attacks, or short-term insomnia. I had been abusing them for nearly six months by that time, and when I didn't have them, I began to get withdrawal symptoms within six hours of my last dose. Pain pills (opiates) and benzos were tough to come by because I needed a prescription, and I was doing everything I could to find doctors who would readily dole them out.

Alcohol, of course, was easy to come by. Even when the liquor stores were closed, I'd go to the grocery store to buy cooking sherry and pound it down. Hiding bottles had become a sort of game for me, and trying to hide my addiction became an everyday affair. I hid from everybody, but especially from my wife. I stashed the bottles above the ceiling panels in my basement. I rotated where I put the bottles, so Carol wouldn't know I'd been drinking. I shoved bottles behind the freezer in the garage. I stuffed them in an old hunting duffle bag. I even managed to get up—early, when I first started to get the shakes—and polish off the rest of a bottle, then walk in my underwear down the alleyway to toss the empty in a neighbor's garbage can. I made sure to conceal the bottle properly under some trash, of course. Clandestine bottle disposal was one of my talents. Lying was more than just second nature; it became who I was. Dishonesty was my identity, my well-earned modus operandi. Alcohol wasn't my favorite drug, not by far, but since it worked when I needed to have *something*, I kept getting it.

For all the drinking I did, the pills were what I really wanted. My stomach had started to bleed when I drank, and my gut hurt every time I did. It was painful but not enough to stop me. Opiates were my poison of choice, but benzos were okay too when I couldn't get the pain pills. Pills seemed to do the job so much cleaner than alcohol. The doctors in town had begun to catch on to my game though. From one doctor to the next, I had the same ploy: get what I need, use, and get more. When I couldn't, I'd return to liquor, despite its damaging effect on my body and mind.

Whether pills or booze, it didn't matter—they stopped working like they had in the years when I first headed down this dubious path. I still needed them, though. But it was to stave off any impending withdrawal, not to get high. The shakes and the anxiety would subside, just for a bit. However, my respites from the aches and pains—both physically and mentally—got shorter and shorter. I learned later that this merry-go-round has a scientific description. Scientists call it physiological dependence. In my brain, the regulatory neurotransmitter GABA wasn't working correctly, at least without the presence of alcohol or benzodiazepines. When GABA functions as it should in a brain, a person can relax when it is appropriate—such as right before bedtime. Since I had abused drugs that modulated the amount of GABA in my brain, my brain chemistry changed as a reaction and I became tolerant to the effect of alcohol or drugs. When the chemicals weren't in my system, my brain said, "Hey! What the hell happened?! I've got too much activity here!"

What that meant for me was that I felt extremely anxious, and *nothing* I did in the short term made that feeling go away, except drinking or taking more pills. Since I am already an anxious person, those times without my booze or my pills were tough. I felt extremely high-strung and discontent, and I was at risk for seizures. (I had seized earlier that year in the hospital because of my abuse of another drug that causes seizures in overdose, Tramadol.)

When I was arrested the second time, I had run short on my pills, and I had not drunk anything that morning. With-drawal was coming. The deputies took me, handcuffed in the back seat of the SUV, to the Williams County Jail. It sits in a basement with no windows, the only light emanating from bare fluorescent bulbs. One light flickered, snapping on and off. The flashing ate into my nerves, devouring any possibility for serenity. I was terrified what would happen to me. This fact was only magnified by the uncooperative nature of my brain in a state of withdrawal.

A secure elevator accessible only through the locked law enforcement office doors is the sole access point for the basement jail from the ground floor. The elevator is big, maybe for transporting multiple suspects, I don't know. It seemed cavernous and I felt very alone. I hated the deputies. I thought that *they* were the bad guys. Of course, they were doing their jobs and I was no different from any other common criminal they dealt with on a continual basis. We stepped in and the doors closed.

"Are you feeling suicidal, Mr. Maurer?" the male officer asked me.

"Yes," I answered. That was a lie and I knew it.

The female detective looked at the male officer. The elevator bumped as it began to go down. It was going down into a pit of no return, it seemed.

"Um … do you really feel that way? I mean, do you have a plan, Dan?" the detective asked me.

"I don't know. I just don't want to live anymore. I don't have any way to get out of this," I said.

The detective pursed her lips and looked down. She didn't need to ask anything more. I had given her my answer and there was a procedure to follow. I wondered what her lack of expression meant. I was trying to manipulate the situation. *Did I give the right answer?*

The sheriff's deputies took me to a room where they processed me. Following their lead, I stood facing the camera. Then they took a side shot. They took me to a machine on a wheeled cart that looked like a high-tech bar scanner. A little glass plate had an outline of a hand in white.

"Place your hand on the outline," one of the deputies said. I complied.

An emerald light came on from underneath the glass plate and the line of light scanned my hand. So now, my prints are digitally scanned, stored away in a federal database somewhere. I was surprised they didn't actually use ink to take fingerprints.

In any other state of mind, the techie-nerdy side of me would have thought the apparatus in front of me was pretty cool. Yet at the time all I wanted to do was make a phone call to my wife or lawyer to get me the hell out of there.

The deputies left. I was alone with the jailers. They had their own procedures to follow. They stripped me down to nothing. Donning latex gloves, they searched where they needed to search. I remember holding back tears. During the whole process, their faces were like stone. I'm sure they were trained well enough to know to keep their attention focused on anything that might go wrong. I mean, I know they'd dealt with their fair share of drunks and criminals, and I could see where a suspect who resisted could upend everything. I didn't resist, but I wasn't happy, either. Today, I don't envy them or hold any resentment for their actions; they were following a routine. They needed to protect themselves and me. At the time, though, I hated their guts, and I remember thinking that what they were doing constituted a war crime. I had to create a bigger deal out of something than it really was. The drama had swallowed me up and I was fully immersed in the hysteria of the moment. In my view, I thought I was the "victim." (In treatment, I'd learn that this pattern of behavior has a name: histrionic personality disorder.)

Then I got my "clothes."

"Here you go. Put this on," the shorter, fatter jailer told me.

"Why do I have to wear this?" I asked.

"Put it on!" His eyes opened wide, and his eyebrows furled.

Fear took hold. Even though I was already in a state of hyper-vigilance, there must be different levels of fear. This one was at a visceral, animal level. My skin felt icy, clammy. My eyes must have been like two, hollow holes glaring back at the jailer. I complied. I took the smock and drew it on, placing my feet first and pulling it up to my torso.

The jailers took me to a cell. I was surprised to see there weren't any metal bars. It goes to show how naïve I was, going into the whole situation thinking it would be like a Western: Sheriff John catches a bad guy. He throws him in the slammer with iron bars and a little open window where birds fly and perch to sing a song of hope to the imprisoned. Then the prisoner gets out quickly, because his lawyer, his wife, *someone* comes to the rescue.

The door was solid metal, painted buff white, and didn't have any edges or corners where a suspect could get hurt. A little window (with shatterproof glass, no doubt) allowed me to see the wall opposite the cell painted in the same drab color. The room itself was a 10x10 box. A stainless steel, seatless urinal sat in the middle of the far wall. An edgeless sink stood directly next to it. These two fixtures were my only companions. The door shut and I heard the electric, mechanical lock snap in the cold metal doorframe.

And I figured it out. I had told the detectives I was suicidal. *So that's why I'm wearing this stupid, uncomfortable smock!* If a guy is really feeling suicidal it's for his protection. That thing was indestructible. A prisoner doesn't have the option to tear apart the fabric and fashion a makeshift noose. Alternatively, if a guy is trying to manipulate the system, if a prisoner says that he doesn't want to live in the hopes that he can get himself out of the hell he finds himself, or if he's begging to go to a psych ward in a hospital instead of a jail cell, then the smock is punishment.

I wanted out. I believed that it was all some mistake, that what I had done in a semi-blackout state wasn't my fault. After all, I needed help, not punishment!

Today I see everything that happened in a different light. The "punishment" of the smock, the cold cell, and the inevitable horror that I had been caught—that experience was the bottom I needed to put me on a path of recovery. I couldn't see it then. I was too pissed off that there wasn't a way out—other than the hard truth. I had to give up the cycle of using and lying, manipulating and stealing, if only to use once again. Giving up was the first step toward true honesty. Giving up meant willingness to try something else, to have the courage to look at myself and say, "Yes, I'm willing to look at things for how they really are and accept them." I needed the honesty, and the courage to give up.

I wasn't ready to give up immediately and I wasn't ready to embrace honesty right away. I did pray though. Man, did I pray! It was the prayer of a frantic, middle-class, and first-world guy to a god (lowercase 'g') who he thought would listen to him. If I could only pray the *right* prayer, if I could really *mean* it this time—then I would be a good boy. It was a cry of desperation to a god who gives out favors to people who come to that god only as a last resort. Unfortunately, that's the only time people come to this god. It was a foxhole prayer to a Santa Claus god, a figure who takes away the pain of the moment and makes everything right again, doling out party gifts to believers in their time of need. Interestingly, that god is a lot like drugs. He works instantly, right when you need him the most, supposedly bringing everything back into focus. Just like drugs, that god was easy to tuck away until you need him again.

That god doesn't exist. He never has. My game of dishonesty was just a hustle with myself. I was still standing in the empty cell with a stainless-steel toilet and sink as my company and I was still wearing that damned smock. I put my plans away to try to manipulate the staff. I was there and that was that. There was nothing I could do about it.

I was in that cell for about twenty-four hours. I must have had three, maybe four hours of sleep that night. It wasn't fun. The fluorescent lights weren't pleasant either. The jailers kept them on constantly, probably more for the nearly constant stream of new prisoners who needed to be processed. Williston, North Dakota, was at the height of the oil boom, and booms tend to both produce economic success and draw shady characters willing to make a quick buck illegally. It was the Wild West. Of course, with those who chose to earn their money an honest way, they could always drink their profits away in the many establishments catering to them, and many oil workers did. Rest assured some would try to drive home. Those unlucky dopes would inevitably fall into the hands of the law, which were already full with all the crime the boom had afforded them.

With all the commotion and the lights, sleep didn't come easily that night. I have a tough time relaxing in general, but insomnia has a magnifying effect when a person is withdrawing from alcohol and benzos. It wasn't the worst part of it. Boredom and my inability to do anything to affect my situation were the toughest things. I was all about control, and my lack of it in that place bothered me greatly. Whatever happened in my life with my addiction, I believed to that point that I could *manage*. But in that cell, I couldn't even manage to distract myself effectively. The minutes seemed to drag by. I couldn't see a clock through the window and there obviously wasn't one in the cell. The staff by then had quit answering my calls to them from the little call button near the door. I had asked—multiple times—when I could speak with my wife. Or my lawyer. Or what their plan was for me. I didn't know how to make the time pass more quickly.

I asked for reading material. They wouldn't have it. I asked for a Bible. After one or two hours, they finally relented with that request. I got a little New Testament with a fake leather, orange plastic cover, like the one I had been given as a kid by door-to-door missionaries. I think it was a King James Version. *Whatever. It was something.*

I suppose part of me believed that my special-favors Santa Claus-of-a-god would look kindly upon his servant, who in his difficulty was looking to Holy Scripture. I had turned to scripture in the past. Believed it, even, as best I could. At least I assume the people in my parish thought that their pastor had sufficient training in seminary to understand, interpret, and convey God's Word to them.

You see, until the day I was arrested and thrown into a 10x10, fluorescent-lit box wearing only a green anti-suicide smock, accompanied only by a stainless-steel sink and a lidless toilet as accruements, I was an ordained pastor in the Evangelical Lutheran Church in America (ELCA).

I know that addiction affects all types of people. Lawyers, doctors, engineers, homemakers, politicians, construction workers, nurses, cops, businessmen and women, rock stars, homeless, and yes, pastors too. No one is immune to the possibility that they have a brain susceptible to the claws of addiction. For me, it was that much more humiliating that I—a supposedly spiritual person and a leader of a congregation—had sunk to a spiritual low-point, thinking it was a good idea to sneak into others' homes to look for drugs.

I was in a box, literally and figuratively, and I saw no way out. Think of it this way: normally when you read a book, you know that the plot will take twists and turns. You read to the climax of the story. You look at the page number and brush your thumb over what pages still remain. With my story, it's like my addiction ripped the rest of the pages away from my life's story. In a Williams County jail cell, I thought my story was done. Dishonesty had gotten me to that point, and there was only one thing that would get me out—honesty.

Honesty

I had been to AA meetings before my arrest. At that time, I hated going to them. In particular, one passage from the Big Book (the basic text of Alcoholics Anonymous) bugged me: "Rarely have we seen a person fail who has thoroughly followed our path. Those who do not recover are people who cannot or will not completely give themselves to this simple program, usually men or women who are *constitutionally incapable of being honest with themselves*" (Emphasis mine.)[1]

I wondered whether I was one of those people.

My track record should have been proof enough that dishonesty was getting me nowhere; I'd always end up drinking again, complicating the problem further. Maybe I'd even drink so much I'd vomit. Then I'd swear off drinking or drugging for the next day. Yet, a new day would come and I'd do it all over again. Dishonesty is insidious; it creeps in your mind and you believe the lies as truth. Before I got sober, I put the fear that I might never be able to be honest with myself out of my mind. Not thinking about it was easier. Alcohol and drugs were a perfect match for not thinking about my life, or anything else. It's easy to forget when you're blasted.

Getting honest with myself was hard, but it was an easier process than getting arrested, nearly losing my family, and

---

[1] AAWS, Inc. 2001. *Alcoholics Anonymous.* 4th ed. New York, NY. Alcoholics Anonymous World Services, Inc. 58.

spending nearly $100,000[2] trying to get sober. For people like me, hitting rock bottom was a prerequisite for being able to listen closely enough to what the program has to teach about honesty. It doesn't need to be that way. But for most people, unfortunately, it is, because it's human nature to be dishonest when we think it benefits us.

Mark Twain once wrote in a notebook that honesty was the best of all the lost arts. I think what he meant is that human beings are not naturally honest, that honesty takes work. I often struggled with honesty growing up. I remember when I was a kid, I was in the garage and I really, really had to go to the bathroom. I didn't think that I could make it, so I went in the corner of the garage. Later that day, my parents discovered my deed. My Dad asked me what I had done. I told him that the dog must have relieved himself there. Well, there was no way our little dachshund could have done that. My Dad punished me, not only for doing what I'd done, but also for lying. My response was interesting. I remember feeling regret, but it wasn't regret for what I had done. It was regret that I had told such an unbelievable lie. I promised myself with a vigorous new commitment that I would be more creative and believable the next time around. Instead of doing the easier work learning honesty by facing my shame, I chose to double down by endeavoring to be all the more clever.

I think a lot of alcoholics and addicts have the same problem with honesty, but I can speak only for myself. My struggle with honesty had its roots in my shame. Shame is the belief that it's not just your actions that are bad: it's that *you yourself* are bad. One solution is to bury that belief and to keep burying it deeper

---

[2] One of my assignments at treatment was to enumerate the financial cost of my addiction. After adding together money I'd spent on three treatments, the alcohol and drugs I had consumed, and the psychologists I visited, that total was close to this figure. Today, I count it as tuition for the privilege of living as a person in recovery.

with lies you tell yourself—heaping on more lies, tossing dirt to entomb your identity within a deep hole. Soon you don't realize how deep reality is buried, how hidden it has become from what you believe to be true about you. For me, as for most people, that solution turned out to be not a solution at all, but instead only something to complicate my life.

The key to honesty for me was embracing my identity as an addict and an alcoholic, claiming it for myself, despite any shame I had. That's what happened when I finally got sober. Shame loves secrecy, but honesty loves acceptance. Shame thrives when it's buried. Honesty thrives when the shame is brought into the light and withers.

Bill W. wrote in *Twelve by Twelve*, "The best we can do, with all the honesty that we can summon, is to try to have it."[3] Honesty is never easy, because it places before a person the way things are, and the-way-things-are isn't always pleasant to look at. Sometimes addressing reality head on is even less pleasant, but it's worth it. Why? Because the-way-things-are is all we ever have. Any fantasy a person has that deviates from the facts—the hard, true facts of life—is bound to send that person deeper into a fiction, and some of the fictions about who-we-are are lies. That I believed that I was one of the good guys, all while I was stumbling around in a blackout looking for other people's pills, was a lie. I victimized people; I hurt them, even while I was hurting myself.

Although the tendency to be dishonest might be more prevalent (and in some ways more acute) among alcoholics and addicts than non-addicts, anyone can benefit from the lessons of the Twelve Steps. In fact, a non-addict gave what is perhaps the greatest gift of freedom for alcoholics and addicts in the

---

[3] AAWS, Inc, 1981. *Twelve Steps and Twelve Traditions.* New York, NY: Alcoholics Anonymous World Services, Inc. and The A.A. Grapevine, Inc. 66.

words of the Serenity Prayer, a prayer repeated in almost every Twelve Step group around the world. The theologian Reinhold Niebuhr perhaps did not foresee that so many men and women would find hope that they could be honest with God's help:

> God, grant me the serenity to accept the things
> I cannot change,
> The courage to change the things I can,
> And wisdom to know the difference.

This simple prayer attributed to Niebuhr is rooted deeply in honesty. It encourages a person to simply accept reality as it is without any pie-in-the-sky fantasies to cloud it. The prayer gently invites us to look at the issue of honesty by first facing the shame that binds us, bringing it into the light of honesty, the things we cannot change—reality. We pray then for God to help us accept that reality. Then, it kills that shame through the power of courage. In the end, all that's left is honesty, the wisdom that true power lies in the work of our Higher Power.

In January of 2011, I thought my life was over. What I didn't yet realize was that it was just beginning, because I was finally willing to be honest with myself.

After my arrest, I entered Hazelden Betty Ford Foundation's treatment facility in Center City, Minnesota. The counselors and the other patients were the people who made a difference for me. The counselors were competent, but their competence in their ability to reach me was more than their skill or training. They were compassionate and empathetic people. At the same time, they were honest with me. Their honesty hurt sometimes. Any sharp redirection in a person's life is bound to be painful. My arrest was a huge redirection; I felt like I was at the bottom of a canyon and the walls were collapsing around me. However, pain is the growth we experience and the treasure we hold onto as we discover and acknowledge where our skewed perspective led us.

I entered Jellinek, the extended-care unit for hardcore cases, after I had been at Hazelden one month. Extended care usually lasts an additional two months beyond the first month of primary treatment. The daily activities with the other residents and the outings we took into the little towns surrounding Hazelden to attend AA meetings became calisthenics for my new, spiritual muscles, which had atrophied from daily drug and alcohol use. Slowly, I began to form a new story for my life. I learned a new narrative and new affirmations about my identity, an identity based in reality, in honesty.

I knew that my Higher Power (and the good within me) could defeat the bad if I were to simply give up and see myself for who I was:

> I am Daniel Maurer, a son who is loved, a husband and father who can show love too, a minister who made a difference, and I'm a gifted communicator and writer. Now, I am also a person of long-term recovery and I accept that. I will always be an addict and an alcoholic. But my weaknesses and my pain can be a gift too. I can give back to others. The truth is that my story is not yet finished.

When I became honest, I saw that there was a life beyond the hell. I began to dream again. The first dream I remember was in my third month in the Jellinek unit at Hazelden. I remember it clearly: I was creating a graphic novel (a big, fat, comic book) illustrating the Twelve Steps. The book showed the concepts of Twelve Step recovery in an artistic format, using the crazy and wildly creative medium of comics to convey real stories to new addicts in recovery. I kept this dream as a new gift to give me a purpose and direction, a hope for the future. It gave me a sense of purpose and meaning for myself, and hope that others might also discover a new spiritual connection to their Higher Power. I also thought that, because of the format, characters' stories would seem more real and relatable.

I took this dream with me to the sober house where I lived in Saint Paul after I had completed my time at the treatment facility in Center City. I connected with an artist, Spencer Amundson, and we began to collaborate, diving deep into how such a story would come together. After two years of work, back with my family and living in Saint Paul, Minnesota, I took the idea to Hazelden Publishing. Eventually, my dream was realized. *Sobriety: A Graphic Novel* came to life in November of 2014, offering hope to other addicts and alcoholics in recovery.

Today, I'm a freelance writer and award-winning author. I'm very grateful for the new life I've been given. I've written and published another book since then. With the blog I keep online,[4] I share not only the experiences of recovering alcoholics and addicts, but also others' stories of personal transformation. I'm fascinated with the process of change and how to make those changes stick.

The horrible experience of my arrest isn't something I'd wish on anyone, but I completely understand why we need law enforcement, and today I'm grateful they arrested me. I would never have dreamt that what happened to me did. I certainly didn't plan on being an addict or ruining my life when I began serving as a pastor. What I know now is that people can change. I did.

Working toward daily sobriety wasn't easy. It still isn't. Sobriety required simple effort on my part. The process is easy to understand: I needed to replace the instinct to control people,

---

[4] *Transformation is Real* at changeisreal.com.

places, things and situations with the will of my Higher Power. What I discovered is that I cannot accomplish the "transfer" of my willpower without first being *honest*. It was very hard work because I needed to confront the shame I had buried so deeply in the first place. I had to look with honesty at my life and face reality. When I embraced honesty and saw that God was changing me, I noticed something unexpected.

Life got easier.

I used to lie about the stupidest things, like when my wife asked me over the phone if I had picked up bananas for the boys at the store. My knee-jerk response? "Yes. I picked up the bananas." Then I hustled to the store and picked up a bunch of nice bananas before she got home. This example seems innocuous, but the issue for me wasn't. It was insidious. The dishonesty wreaked havoc with my relationships because people simply couldn't trust me. Of course, I told other lies that were much bigger, like drinking and drugging, along with the hiding and self-justifications I made from my flimsy attempt at building my own house of cards. I'm grateful today that I am willing to strive for complete honesty, even if some days I need to revisit my old habits. Thankfully, I don't have to strive for an honest life alone.

Life got easier in part because I discovered I wasn't alone. I didn't have to do it all myself. God has worked through other people, like my Twelve Step sponsor, to teach me about honesty. He told me, "Every time you tell a lie, I want you to say, 'No. That is a lie.'" Doing what he asked wasn't fun or easy, but boy, was it effective, especially in those early days when I lived in a sober house in St. Paul. I began to establish a new pattern: I would catch myself on the edge of lying before I did it. I'm not perfect and I still catch myself about to lie. However, ever since I began noticing what I'm about to say, I strive to choose the honest answer. What I find today is that I can much more easily handle the curveballs life throws at me. My stress level is much less than it was. I'm no longer hyper-vigilant. This change is a miracle.

I wouldn't go back to my old ways for anything, because, not only does honesty make life easier, honesty is vital to my recovery. In fact, it's the main asset I can put to work to lead a healthy spiritual life. Honesty is the foundation of my resilience.

When I was living in the post-treatment "pink cloud" of life without chemicals in a crowded sober house in St. Paul, I discovered how honesty could change everything for me. I was bouncing back into life, big time. I could feel and dream again! However, personal transformation isn't just about my experience—the self-induced trauma and stress of my arrest, my recovery from addiction, my newfound joy and gratitude. I shared my success in meetings, and other people told me they had experienced equally favorable outcomes by embracing their own spiritual journey, just as working toward an honest life had made life easier, better, for me. I started sharing non-addicts' stories of transformation and enduring hardships on my website, and gradually I discovered that spiritual assets seemed to contribute positively to every struggler's resilience. I wanted to explore the connection further.

Spiritual Assets and Resilience

Spiritual asset isn't a term we often hear. *Spiritual gift* is more common, especially in some Christian circles. Different Christians view spiritual gifts differently, however. One way to look at them is as a defined list of *charismata* (Greek for "freely given favor") outlined in the New Testament. In the narrowest sense of the term, spiritual gifts could be defined as specific traits that a believer receives from God: knowledge, wisdom, faith, the gift of healing, the gift of miracles, the discernment of spirits, the gift of tongues, and the ability to interpret tongues. Although these gifts have a rich history in various Christian traditions, I'm taking a broader view of *spiritual gifts* as any good gift or virtue that flows from God's love to us.

Spiritual gifts become *spiritual assets* when we use them to nurture our spiritual life. A material asset is a useful item—an object or a "thing"—that a person owns, like a house or a car. You can live in a house or drive a car. You can also use a house or a car as collateral to get a loan. In a similar vein, you can possess a spiritual gift like honesty. Honesty becomes a spiritual asset when you use it to build your connection with God and others.

Spiritual assets share some characteristics:

- *Spiritual assets are dependable.* We can count on them. The assets have a useful purpose for us and they make a difference because they are rooted in the gifts we receive from a Higher Power.

- *We can turn away from spiritual assets and the benefits they give.* You can choose not to use the gifts you've been given as an asset for your spiritual life. For instance, I could choose once again to go back to drinking and drugging and return to all the hiding and lying that went with it.[5]

- *Spiritual assets allow us to see more clearly, love more deeply, and act more courageously.* Spiritual assets bring us closer to our spiritual center, to our Higher Power, to God.

---

[5] I choose to believe that my Higher Power, the Infinite One, works within me to choose otherwise.

- *Spiritual assets make us more resilient to the trauma and difficult experiences life inevitably throws at us.* Since spiritual assets bring us closer to our Higher Power, we do not face the difficulties alone, and we may find a greater purpose and meaning within the stress. When we lean on our spiritual assets to get us through, the traumatic event becomes less destructive. Instead, it becomes transformative; we see the difficulties in a new light.

Honesty is a spiritual asset for me because it enables me to lead a centered, healthy life, especially during stressful times. Instead of hiding, I strive to live openly, mistakes and all. Instead of fabricating a story to fit a reality I would like, I'm compelled to look at reality as it is, even though it may scare me. The effects of honesty were immediate for me. When I was crying in a jail cell alone, I had to face the facts about who I was—a lying, manipulative, out-of-control addict. I was able to see that had to give up trying to control life and face the truth that I had hurt others with my behavior.

A person might think that giving up would feel like failure. It wasn't that way for me. For me, it was a relief! My arrest was God's way of giving me two messages: I had to be accountable for my actions, and I didn't need to hide any longer. That meant that no matter what had happened—or what *might* happen—I could proceed with my head high, with honesty.

Embracing honesty as a spiritual asset meant that I didn't need to worry about my ultimate fate; I know that God loves me with all my frailties and weakness. For me, this has to do with confronting my shame. Since I know God loves me, warts and all, I don't have to try to hide or live in my shame. I tried through dishonesty to create an alternate reality that was more acceptable, one in which I'd be *okay*. Now, I go forward in honesty, seeking progress, not perfection, realizing I'm okay to begin with. I'm human and I make mistakes.

Honesty is a spiritual asset I own and I use. It has made me stronger. I don't have to lie, manipulate, or try to finagle my way out. I can trust God. I know that I don't have to control outcomes and try to be the center of everything—because I am not the center. God is. The difficulties I face in life don't seem to affect me as they did before. I have discovered I am *resilient* in the face of stress and trauma.

Resilience is a person's capacity to "bounce back" after a difficult or traumatic experience. It's more than just a person's ability to adapt to stress. Rather, anyone can learn adaptations that may contribute to an ongoing process of recovery. One adaptation in particular is *acknowledging and identifying spiritual assets* that we may use to help us get our lives back.

The consensus among psychologists is that resilience isn't a particular trait only certain people have. Instead, researchers believe that any person can learn or at least become more aware of his or her capacity for resilience. In fact, many people discover their resilience within the stressful event itself.

I know I did.

When I discovered that honesty wasn't as scary as I thought it would be, I began to change my life in the ways I needed to. I also discovered that I was emotionally tougher and more pliable than I ever imagined. I discovered the power of honesty to propel me to deal with life on life's terms instead of my own.

Resilience is a process everyone can participate in, rather than a quality or characteristic possessed by only a select few.[6] Everyone can discover the gifts God freely gives them, and put those gifts to work. Spiritual assets like honesty, gratitude, faith, courage, forgiveness, perseverance, imagination, integrity,

---

[6] Rutter, Michael. 2008. "Developing Concepts in Developmental Psychopathology" In *Developmental Psychopathology and Wellness: Genetic and Environmental Influences*: James J. Hudziak. 3–22. Washington, DC: American Psychiatric Publishing.

service and hope all contribute to our *resilience* following stress or trauma.

I'm still considering just how much my faith or spirituality may contribute to my own resilience to stress or change. I know that sometimes when I catch myself feeling like I used to think—fearful, shame-ridden, or driven to manipulate outcomes—I also, thankfully, feel the pull of the new recovery life beckoning me to return. Now honesty, one spiritual asset among others, is at the center of my new life.

I've often wondered how people I've heard about in the news got through a crisis in one piece. What did they do? What resources did they have? How did the discovery of a spiritual asset contribute to a positive outcome for that person? Does a person's spiritual experience outshine their biology in their ability to bounce back? How do spiritual assets make a difference to anyone during a stressful time? How do spiritual assets influence a person's resilience? Perhaps you have questions like these too.

Spiritual assets can be valuable tools to cultivate grit, character, and the ability to bounce back. *Resilience.* In each of the chapters, the stories are raw and real. Some might make you feel uncomfortable. They have value for us in how they illuminate just which asset(s) that person found within (or after) his or her harrowing experience. Some of the stories aren't about just one specific event, but instead lay out a series of events, a cascade of heartbreak, frustrations, and difficulties.

Here's the thing: people can get through the worst of it. I believe in God's promise that no one's story is ever finished; everyone can discover assets from a higher source. Amazingly, these spiritual assets never let us down, even when we might think otherwise. The benefit is more than many of us who have endured stress could have imagined. I offer my own continuing story as one example.

When I was in my third month of inpatient treatment at

Hazelden Betty Ford's facility in Center City, Minnesota, I took a walk out in the woods. The facility at Center City is blessed with extensive grounds with winding paths leading through thick woods. Several lakes touch the edge of the forest and a path leads close to the shore. It was early June and the budding leaves and the regular cadence of the waves on the lakeshore beamed the optimism that only spring can provide. I breathed in deeply. I felt hopeful. I suppose the founders of Hazelden believed the halcyon setting would stimulate reflection and re-evaluation. That certainly was its effect on me. That evening I wandered by a clutch of trees. I was completely alone. I turned to my left and saw a newborn fawn tucked away beneath the newly blossoming undergrowth. Since I love the outdoors and have spent countless hours in the woods, I had seen baby deer before. This time was different. A hope, of a promise maybe, percolated inside me and bubbled up. I saw what life is: rebirth, renewal, and change. I didn't have to be afraid of the pain or the loss of life, even though I will go through these things. Everyone will. I could reach for honesty and try to live an honest life. I could give back to the world in spite of all the pain I gave others and myself. That moment was my rebirth.

Today, I wake early to get my two boys off to school in the morning and settle into the routine of writing in my home studio. Sometimes I write for my blog, contributing stories of transformation or posting others'. Other times, I rack my brain to come up with a new idea for a gathering activity for a kids' Sunday school educational resource, (which is almost a trauma in its own right). Another day I'll create a science curriculum for K-2nd grades, or write a devotional for a publication. I also write books; I've created two graphic novels and penned an exposé-memoir of a victim's story of human trafficking. Now I'm writing my fourth book.

These gifts of writing, reading, sharing, connecting, living— all rich blessings—continue to raise my spirit every day. I almost can't believe how good life has become, all because of honesty, the asset that restores my perspective and redirects my willingness to keep searching for a greater purpose from outside myself, a spiritual purpose to pass on what I've learned to you. I'm grateful for my recovery, and even more for the opportunity to write. I'm hopeful that this collection of others' accounts will give you your own insight to find your spiritual assets, to awaken your resilience and your ability to overcome whatever obstacles life may bring to you. Transformation is real, and the endurance to persevere dwells within each of us.

Chapter One

Gratitude

I knew Cathy Riley when I was growing up in Anoka, Minnesota, but only through her older brother, Chris. Chris and I both played the trumpet in the high school band and during summers marched together in parades throughout the state. Chris also participated in my wedding as a groomsman. I believe I had met his sister two or three times, but only in passing through my brother, Joe. They had similar interests in high school, mostly partying.

When I began researching and interviewing people for this book, Cathy was recuperating in a hospital in Mississippi. Her story began to interest me when I heard about the trauma she endured and the speed of her recovery. Her sister-in-law told me Cathy was interested in speaking with a writer. We connected and she shared her experience with me.

It has only been ten months since her life's trajectory radically changed. I'm taken by the resiliency of the human body; she looks remarkably healthy, considering what she endured. What strikes me more is how she found a new purpose and spiritual direction that is fundamentally different from the Cathy I knew in high school. She has changed.

When I met with her after not having seen her for nearly 25 years, the first thing I noticed was the way she talks. She speaks today with a distinct southern lilt, and it took me by surprise.

1

This wasn't the young woman I remembered who spoke with a Minnesota accent. I also noticed that she was calm as she recounted her harrowing story. Again, considering what she has been through, her demeanor surprised me. From what little I remember from before, she used to be anxious and uptight. That wasn't my impression when I met with her again.

Cathy and I have different theological beliefs. As a Southern Baptist, her spiritual growth was shaped by a more fundamentalist and evangelical faith. I come from a liberal Lutheran perspective, and I received my theological training as an ELCA pastor. However, she shared her experience with me from a non-judgmental standpoint. The dialogue was constructive, and I felt like she was more interested in finding common ground instead of lifting up our differences. I'm humbled and honored to share her story with you.

Cathy's Story

I was born in Springfield, Ohio, into an upper-middle-class family with two professional parents and an older brother named Chris. My father was a member of Mensa and eventually secured a master's degree and a job as a corporate comptroller. He entertained people with his dry sense of humor until he died in January of '08. My Mom was an LPN and worked full time my whole life. She still works long hours today.

Our first home was a duplex and my parents owned both halves. My brother and I shared a room and had bunk beds. I thought I was so cool and my parents provided me with anything a little girl could want. The summer before I turned eight, my Dad's job as a comptroller required him to move to the Twin Cities in Minnesota. I was scared to move, to leave everything I knew in Ohio and move up north where I didn't know anybody. Dad promised to get us a snowmobile. We packed up everything in a big van and off we went to Anoka, Minnesota, a third-ring suburb north of Minneapolis. This was in 1982. We never did get a snowmobile.

In Minnesota, the area we lived in had plenty of young families and kids stuffed the neighborhood and spilled out into the quiet roads during the summer. Those summer days were long and filled with games. I remember running around neighbors' yards and in their houses, playing tag or hide-and-go-seek. Minnesota hadn't turned out as bad as I had thought. Life was good.

I went to Franklin Elementary for my third and fourth grades. I remember having a lot of friends and liking my teachers. Our parents spoiled us, even though we hadn't gotten our promised snowmobile. I do remember wanting more affection and attention than my brothers. I guess I was the high-maintenance daughter. I had perfect attendance in school and got good grades. Somehow, though, through all of my fond memories, my Mom thought I didn't seem happy. One day, she sent me to see a therapist named Millie. The appointments bored me. It seemed like we only had generic conversations. I don't think anything relevant ever came from my visits with her. I mention her because it wouldn't be the last time I saw a therapist.

Our family belonged to St. Stephens Catholic Church in Anoka, but we only went on Christmas Eve and Easter. I assume my father was the only official member since my older brother and I never completed CCD. The Bible was never out on display or used as a reference in the home and we didn't pray, either at bedtime or at meals.

After I transitioned to middle school, my life began to change.

In sixth grade, some kids called my nose a "ski jump." My nose always had a bump on it and I grew to despise it. (Later in life I had surgery to correct it.) I had always been a bossy kid and I think the other kids knew that all too well. One day there was a revolt against me. The last day of school our class walked to a park. It was sunny and I felt excited for summer vacation. The other kids made up a song about me and they chanted it (endlessly) as we walked back to the school:

> *Cathy Riley is a dog,*
> *Look at her nose; it's a log,*
> *Watch her suck on a fat corn-dog!*

From that day on, it wasn't as fun anymore to live in Anoka, Minnesota. I remember wishing I was back in Ohio.

Seventh grade brought with it new ways to get bullied. The school counselor called me down to her office and asked if I knew about what was going on. I must have had a blank look on my face because I had to ask her before she'd talk.

"What do you wanna tell me?" I asked.

The counselor looked concerned, her eyebrows ruffled. "Other kids are passing around a notebook they're supposed to sign," she said.

"What are they signing?"

"They're supposed to sign it if they don't like you. Most of the class has signed it and I wanted you to know about it. I've taken it away though."

Oh, the joys of pubescence.

My heart sank. I still wonder why she'd told me. Wouldn't it have been okay to simply confiscate the notebook and not tell me? I remember worrying a lot about what was going to happen in life, not thinking about where I was in the moment. There were other times I was bullied, but by then, I had decided that I'd handle everything differently.

My older brother Chris was the golden boy through high school. By then our relationship had soured. I thought there was no sense in trying to get praise through my schoolwork. My younger brothers were so much younger than me that I didn't need to compete with them. I didn't know where I was supposed to fit in. Since I didn't want to come in second place, I decided I'd throw out the schoolbooks and the family time and turn to partying. I'd be a black sheep. The "bad girl." It seemed to work. I followed a clique who liked the new me.

From then on, if I didn't have plans from Friday when school let out through Sunday night, I thought my weekend was wasted. Ninth grade was a doozy: the whole school found out when, where, and with whom I lost my virginity. And of course, the boy dumped me right away. That year I cracked under the constant shame of classmates' name-calling. I went into a deep depression, started skipping school, and even felt suicidal. So off I went to the adolescent psych ward.

There I met an interesting mix of tortured souls: boys who talked to themselves in a corner, girls with eating disorders, kids who had been physically and sexually abused, one boy who cut himself with a scissor on his arm, and one kid who had supposedly molested his two younger sisters. I felt guilty taking up a bed when all I was ... was sad. As alien as I felt at my school, in that place I felt perfectly normal. After all, wasn't I from an all-American family portrayed in a Norman Rockwell painting?

I had a few serious relationships in high school; they lasted close to a year each. I worked part time, was a competitive dancer, attended cosmetology school while completing my senior year at Anoka Senior High. Parties were a priority. My schoolwork was not. I managed to complete what they required from me and I graduated.

After graduation, I lived with a friend and her kids in her apartment, then with another friend and her family. In 1992, I rented the basement in a family friend's home. That year I started hanging around a rougher crowd. Some of the guys were in (or claimed to be in) gangs. Two guys I knew got killed that year. It all came to a head when another friend confessed to murdering a family. I saw him that night. He had bandages on his hands. He came over to my guy friend's house and he wanted us to go riding with him but we had somewhere to be, thank God. Some friends got in the car he was driving. (It actually was the victim's vehicle.) They got pulled over shortly thereafter and they all got arrested. I had to make statements to the police.

Around this time a mentor friend that I had worked for in the neighboring town of Coon Rapids had moved to her home state of Mississippi and was running a little beauty shop in Natchez. She called to ask me if I wanted to move down south and give it a try. She had a place for me to live and a job. She would pay my way down if I would try it out for a couple of months and with everything going on with my social crowd the answer was easy. I moved to Mississippi.

I matured and thrived in my new environment. I had no old baggage holding me back from making improvements in my life. I met some amazing life-long friends and was introduced to my first husband. We dated long distance then I moved three hours south of Natchez to Gulfport, Mississippi, where he had a successful computer business. Brian was a great guy, showered me with attention and had a knack for creative gifts and well-planned surprises. We started to grow our family immediately. Soon, I had the gift of two daughters: Cassidy in '95 and Courtney '96. We married in '96. After four years together, I decided we were cheating ourselves by not being madly and passionately in love and I decided to get my own apartment. I regret separating from him because he was a decent guy. I guess my heart pulled me to be wild, to find something new. I had a habit of worrying about the future. The future I wanted never seemed to come. I was still searching.

One thing gave me rest: my newfound faith. I was saved in '96.

Brian and I went to a Baptist church in Gulfport. He grew up that way and I thought our girls should be raised in a church. At first, I didn't know what to think about it all. I had never gone to church as a kid, just for major holidays. Also, I was Catholic, at least in name. I didn't care about that though; the place was nice and the people welcomed me into their fellowship. I decided to give it a try.

After attending service for a while, they had an altar call. Something was pulling me to come forward. I knelt and I started to cry. It seemed like in that moment I finally felt like I belonged, that God was real and I could find the meaning and direction I was searching for. Soon they scheduled a baptism for me. Down South, they do full immersion. When the day came and the pastor thrust my body below the water, I had a vision of Jesus on the cross, dying for my sins. I felt—at least in that moment—accepted. I accepted Jesus into my heart that day.

I started going regularly to church. The teachers for the adult Sunday school gave me answers to the questions I had, like: Did Adam and Eve have belly buttons? Or what about the dinosaurs? Did they exist and how long has the world been around? They gave me simple answers from the Bible. I guess I needed that at the time.

After the divorce, I had a few serious relationships. I was engaged twice. None of the guys were ever abusive, because I would have never put up with that. That's what I thought I believed anyway. I kept going to church occasionally, although some folks seemed to look down on me because I was divorced.

The first time I met my abuser, Richie, I thought he was a bad boy with nice muscles. That was in 2001. He had just gotten out of prison and moved to Biloxi from Las Vegas. He was the brother of my friend Tiffany. We made out in a club one night. At the time I was working in a casino in Biloxi and my friend worked with me. She warned me her brother was an asshole, and that I was too good for him. I was interested, I think, because he was bad; he seemed fun. By that time I returned to my old ways, partying, drinking and trying to have fun. Soon after, he ended up getting someone else pregnant. (That woman actually called me and asked me to stay away from him.) I didn't see or talk to him until later. Fast-forward seven years when Tiffany fell sick. She died two weeks later of Hodgkin's lymphoma.

That year, 2008, turned out to be the worst year of my life. My dad died that January. A close friend who had been my Sunday school teacher when I got saved passed in March. An end came to my three-year engagement to another man. And then on March 31st, my beautiful and full-of-life friend Tiffany died of cancer. By mid-April, Richie had abandoned his girlfriend and her two older kids. Before I knew what had happened, he moved in with my two daughters and me. He had one five-year-old son from his most recent relationship and another, a six-and-a-half-year-old boy who thought Richie was his dad. (He also had a daughter with a previous relationship. Richie got around—he spread his bloodline far and wide for sure.) The drinking flowed for both of us and the bickering was immediate. I guess we were grieving together—now I've learned there's a name for this, a *trauma bond*. He was not exactly the type I usually went for. But there we were, living together, a family.

My abuser was a caveman with a loud voice and no social skills. He was always breaking stuff in anger—smashing cell phones, the dinner table chairs, the visor of my car, and the driver's side window of my SUV. I have come to learn he displayed all of the red flags of being an abuser. However, I didn't know it then. I thought that he'd get over it, that he had just never found the right person. All the relationships he had in the past had been strippers and druggies. I was different. I thought he'd change. But this was a man with a lot of baggage. He had been charged and convicted not only of domestic violence, but also of grand larceny and weapons charges. I kept staying with him, night after night, even with all the yelling and smashing.

He was a heavy drinker and often when he drank he accused me of screwing around. He always was suspicious of me, checking my phone … and doing worse. One night in September of 2008, after I had recently completed a job where I managed real estate, condos, I had been to a going-away dinner the company threw for me. When I came home, I could smell the liquor in the house. The smell seemed to fill an invisible bubble around him. I knew that something was going to happen, but I thought it wasn't anything I couldn't handle. But then Richie said, "Who've you been sleeping with?!"

"Nobody!" That was the truth.

"Bullshit. Let me check you."

I couldn't believe it. He wanted me to pull down my pants and physically "check" to see if I'd been having sex. I resisted and we got in a fight. It was the first time that he became physically abusive with me. He punched me multiple times viciously in the head and forced me down on the couch. He pummeled me in the head where my hair would cover the bruises.

"This is what you deserve, bitch!"

He started to pull down his pants. I was afraid he was going to rape me. But he did something worse: he urinated on me.

We fought some more and I tried to leave to go to the doctor and check out my lumps and bumps. He wouldn't let me leave. He forced me down on the bed and slept on top of me so I couldn't leave. The next morning, he left for work at 4 a.m. He believed me when I told him I'd be fine and he got ready to leave. It was my first experience with domestic violence and I couldn't believe it happened to me. I had the courage to call a friend after he left and she took me to the police department. I pressed charges.

That day, I left to stay at a friend's house. I don't know why he didn't get charged right away, but I think it had something to do with his official address at his parents' place. Maybe it just got lost in a shuffle of papers, who knows? But pretty soon he was trying to weasel his way back into my life.

I thought, *maybe I overreacted. Maybe the police don't see it the way I do. Maybe this is the way it's supposed to be.* Of course, he apologized and said he needed anger management. I found out by October that he'd been cheating on me, that I got an STD from him, and that I was pregnant. In December of '08, I had a miscarriage. That year was a train wreck, a complete tornado. As I look back on that year, I know what the sensible thing to do would have been to run. Run away. Run anywhere but with him.

Instead, we got married.

I was so beat down. I think I had a nervous breakdown. Staying with him seemed like a solution, even though it condemned me to more misery.

In July of '09, we moved outside Jackson, Mississippi in a little town named Pearl. And I was pregnant again. That one stuck and later that year I gave birth to my son, Lincoln. Then in 2010, the charges that I had pressed on him from before (in Biloxi) came to life and the authorities started chasing him down. The physical abuse continued, only he didn't hit me. Instead, he choked me and grabbed me by my arms and shoved me to the floor. Of course, the psychological abuse dragged on. He berated me daily and told me what a whore I was and how I was trying to ruin his life with the domestic violence charges.

All the while, I was seeing a counselor through the police station. I told them that I needed help and they asked me if I wanted to go to a shelter. I refused because I still thought I could handle him. When I went home, it was a different story I fed Richie. I told him that I would explain everything in court and it would all work out. I was lying, of course. I wanted him to pay for what he'd done to me, but I didn't want him to take it out on me. I stayed the course I thought I should.

When the court date came, we traveled to Biloxi together.

When we got out of the car to go into the courtroom I remember him saying, "You'd better tell 'em what they need to hear." When the time came to testify, the prosecutor was hard on him. And when the judge read the report, I was crying out of humiliation, because he was reading about Richie peeing on me and everything. I felt like everybody in the courtroom was staring at me, wondering why I'd let the abuse go so far. He ended up getting one-year probation. The judge said that if he laid a pinky on me, he'd throw the book at him. He had to go to anger management twice a week.

The sentence afforded me a bit of safety, because I threatened to call on him when things escalated, which of course they did. But Richie wasn't stupid. Instead of physical violence, he began specializing in the put-downs. The psychological abuse hit me hard. Instead of recognizing my abuser's actions as stereotypical, I started asking myself how I had been the one who messed up my marriage, how I had made him do what he did. He made good money working for waste management, so I also had the fear of providing for my kids without him.

And there were days when things seemed better, that there was hope for a real family, one more like I had grown up with. There were good parts in my life. I had two dogs and a cat that I loved and played with. I remember laughing with my kids. Some days, Richie was okay. By that, I mean he didn't yell or threaten us as much. I kept hoping things would get better. Although Richie's son took some abuse, it was infrequent. Richie yelled at the girls, but never touched them. I wouldn't have stood for that. But by 2012, I decided that I'd make our marriage as miserable as possible, so he'd want to leave too. I fought back with my words, putting him down as hard as he did to me. The yelling was constant and our home was a pit of despair. But I didn't feel like I had the option to just leave. I knew he'd track me down. At the same time, I thought that I should make the marriage work somehow. I know now that those two beliefs don't match up—that I would try to make things work, all while trying to make things miserable. I thought that maybe God could change him. I got this idea from the counselors we started seeing at Christian therapy.

At first, we saw seminary students for marriage counseling at a Reformed seminary. We got discounted counseling fees because students were giving us advice. Everything they said was from the Bible. I don't know exactly what verses, but the message was clear: we had to make it work, no matter what. Divorce wasn't an option. I believed it couldn't be an option for me either. They said I should be grateful for the relationship, that what God had brought together no man should separate. I heard the words, "You should be grateful," but I didn't believe them. Who knows what Richie thought? I know after those sessions, he was nice for a bit, but he soon fell back into his old ways.

By 2013, I was deeply depressed and crying myself to sleep at night. I couldn't believe what a wreck my marriage was. I started going to intensive outpatient therapy for twelve weeks at a psychiatric center. My medication for my depression didn't seem to be working and no one would believe me. Eventually, I stabilized and I started another job with Pier One and was working my way up. In the fall of 2013, with the help of the local women's crisis center, I left Richie and took the kids. I did what I thought was right for me and my family. I filed for divorce. He started visiting single's websites.

I lived away for nine months. The holidays were hard; I was lonely. He wasn't signing the divorce papers and I wasn't making the money I was promised. During the time I was away, I started going to my church for advice. The pastor told me exactly what I had heard at the seminary—I had to make the marriage work. Richie eventually came to the sessions. After those times, I could see he always felt good afterwards because he had a smile on his face. It's like he was getting the affirmation he needed. I want to research the issue of marriage in the Bible and all the theology, because it seems to me that "love your neighbor" should apply to marriages too. My abuser didn't love me. Maybe he said it from time to time, but he didn't really love me. I know this now, but at the time, I kept thinking that they were right, that I was wrong, that I had to stay with him and love and cherish him. That meant that I slowly listened to Richie's bullshit that he would change, that things would be different, that it would all work out. I thought that I should be grateful, that I should have gratitude for a house, a husband, a family, and the American dream. So what if he drank too much? So what if he slapped me around? I should be grateful. Still, something tickled the back of my head that told me I should trust what my guts were telling me, that I should leave.

I moved back in with Richie in June of 2014, thinking that God was guiding my steps. I actually said this in an interview in a new job I applied for at a hardware store. I said, "We'll see if I get the job. I believe God's guiding my steps." They were (and are) good people. Believers too. I got the job. Things began to look up. I started to meet a lot of nice, conservative, good, Christian men. Richie always told me that all men were pigs, that they only wanted sex. Women were just as bad in his eyes. He really hated them, even though he always chased after women for sex. The men I met at work weren't pigs though. They were decent people.

We bought a house together. It was a nice, brick house at the end of a cul-de-sac, one like I had lived in when I was a kid in Ohio. Maybe I did this because I thought it would change Richie—getting a home together making a life for us, as it should be. It didn't, of course. So I had to make a decision, a new decision. I had to stick with it too. I thought I had to leave Richie for good, but I wanted to keep my new house. I wanted to have my life to myself. The question I was thinking was how I should go about doing that. I finally made a plan.

After I started the job at the hardware store, I told Richie
that I was going to do what I wanted. I was going to get back
on Facebook and not wear my wedding ring. I was still living
with him, but I had met all these good guys through work.
I knew there could be something else for me, for my family.
Honestly, I thought that I could just go out as friends with
these guys and see where it led. He knew that I was serious
about getting divorced. He'd show up at my job, bawling and
howling, promising that he'd be the husband God wanted him
to be. It was pathetic. And embarrassing. I thought bringing
him to this level would get him fed up enough and finally make
a decision to just ... leave.

On October 1st of 2014, I could see the gophers in his head
spinning a wheel. It was in his eyes. They had that deer-in-a-
headlights look that there was nothing he could do to change
my mind. I was going to make him leave. I would keep the
house and pay him off. I would keep the kids and the pets.
When I told him exactly what my plans were, I saw two things:
his eyes, how desperate and shocked he looked, and I saw his
face, his mouth actually—his lips came tightly together and
I saw him look away. I knew he was plotting something. I
should have taken action right then, but I didn't. I thought I
was in control.

He was out in the yard that evening, drinking hard. I ignored
him and was already in bed with my son, Lincoln watching
cartoons. Lincoln had fallen asleep on my tummy, and I was
drifting off. Richie came into the room and starting yelling at
me: "You fucking cunt! Where's your phone?"

"Why do you wanna see my phone?!"

He demanded to see it.

"Who have you been fucking? Who?!" he yelled. I wouldn't
give it to him.

"You're not getting in my phone even if I give it to you.
I've got it locked." I thought he'd back down and return to his

pity-party in the backyard.

"Gimme the password! Gimme your goddamn phone!"

He kept reaching for it, but I kept pushed him away. He left our room and went to his pickup truck and got a machete. (I only know this now, because I read it later in the confession papers he gave when he was arrested.)

I don't remember a lot of what happened. I had to piece together a lot in my therapy and reading what legal papers I have now. I seem to have blotted most of it out. He snatched me off the bed and I threw the cell phone to my son and screamed to him, "Call 911! Call 911!" I don't blame my son for not calling 911. (I had my cell phone locked. He was only four and didn't know what to do. He'd seen us fight before too, but nothing like that day. I'm sure he was terrified.)

Richie grabbed me by the hair, dragged me into the living room and pushed me down. He hit me on the head with the machete and the blade cut into my scalp. I have extensive defensive wounds on my right hand. He cut off one of my fingers. The papers say he hit me four to five times, but it seems like more, I just can't remember.

The next thing I knew is that I was sprawled out on the floor with blood soaking into the carpet. I see blood splattered on the wall. I felt the blood pouring from my head and I thought, I'm going to die. *That sonofabitch has killed me!* He went into our bedroom. Then I remember him stepping over me with Lincoln in his arms. He said, "Don't look at Mom. Don't look at Mom."

I knew when he went back down the hallway leading to our bedroom I had to snap him out of it, out of his craziness, out of his rage.

"Richie, please! You gotta call 911. You've already done this. I'm gonna die. You can't leave me. I have three children! I'm your wife!" I was in a daze. He stood for a moment. Maybe it surprised him what he'd done.

I was still pleading with him to do the right thing. He walked toward the door to leave.

I knew I didn't have much time. A person has only got so much blood. I knew I had to get help, but I couldn't move.

He didn't say he was sorry. He didn't get me a towel. He left me.

"I'm gonna have to kill myself," were his last words to me.

I heard him shut the door and I'll never forget the sound of the automatic lock we had installed on our front door. Zzzzzz, click, the lock went, sealing me in, forever. He locked me in and left me to die, alone.

I peed and pooped myself. I had heard this happens when you're going to die.

I'm gonna die. All alone here on my floor. I blacked out.

"Break the glass! Break the glass!" I heard somebody yell. *Was that my voice? Was that me?* (It was. But I don't remember saying it. I found out later I yelled for them to break the glass. I thought then someone else was yelling.)

I opened my eyes. I heard the door open. People were in my house. Light shined in my eyes. It was bright. I squinted.

"What did he hit you with?"

"Wha …?"

"What'd he hit you with?!" It was a man's voice.

"A ma … machete."

"A machete?"

I found out later that I said it was a machete. The responding officer had a personal video cam on him (another miracle, I'll get to that), and everything I say about my story and how the attack happened, I've heard on that video. I don't remember what I did, though, especially that I said Richie used a machete. I didn't even know what a machete was. When I came to in the ICU later, I thought it was a samurai sword. The fact I said that it was a machete makes me believe my reactions weren't my own, but something supernatural happened that day. Something came over me to save my life, to give me the words I needed to say. Also, after the cops came in, I looked and sounded calm. There was no hysteria, no screaming. I couldn't believe it myself until I watched the video. The calm seemed to come down on me without me knowing about it. I don't know how to explain it. I believe now that God was there for me, maybe an angel.

"Who did this?" the man asked.

"Richie, my husband. He's got my son. Please go find him. He said he's gonna kill himself."

"You just stay calm. We're getting help."

The EMTs came through the door. In our house, our foyer led to the living room. The foyer floor was wood. The living room was carpeted. Most of the blood spilled out on the carpet, but I could see that it was starting to pool on the wood. There was so much blood. But I was calm. When the EMTs came, I had put my right foot up on a love seat in the living room. I don't know why I did this, but it surprised the EMTs.

"I don't believe this," a man said.

"What?"

"Your vitals are normal. It's a good thing you put your foot up. It's great that you knew to do this."

"Do what?"

"To put your foot up. You've lost a lot of blood, but we're here to help you." I didn't understand what he meant. I was beginning to fade fast. Later I found out that it probably helped save me that day that I put my foot up because it got more blood to my vital organs.

The EMT asked me questions. I felt woozy. It was difficult to concentrate.

"Who's the President of the United States?"

"I … dunno. Bush."

"What's your daughters' phone number?"

I didn't know.

"How many quarters make a dollar?"

"I …"

"Okay. It's okay. You stay calm," one of them said. They were talking to each other, too, about my medical condition. And they were chatting back and forth on a radio, I think. I knew that I had cuts on my head, but I didn't know at the time how big they were. What I know now is that large chunks of my scalp and my skull were missing, exposing my brain tissue.

The EMT bandaged my head. They moved me around, gently. I recall that I was afraid but calm. They loaded me, first on a gurney, then into the ambulance.

"Cathy, can you feel this?" the paramedic in the back asked me.

"Yeah. I feel it. You're poking my leg …" I managed to slur. He seemed surprised that I could feel him poking my leg.

"Okay. Can you move your left arm?" he asked.

I tried to move. I couldn't. I must have whimpered.

"It's okay. We'll get it all figured out." I didn't know what he meant.

Now I know that he was testing to see if I had feeling on my left side, and whether or not I was paralyzed.

"Hurry up … she's fading fast. We gotta get there!" I heard someone say in the ambulance. This worried me. Hadn't they said I was stable?

When we got to the hospital, everything was in a blur. It was like when you put a dab of butter on a hot pancake, first, the butter below melts, and then it all starts to slide around. That's what it felt like in my head like my consciousness was melting. It's like I wasn't all there, but there I was, still.

A nurse came into the room and was trying to get off my earrings. She couldn't seem to get them off.

"I know, these are funny. They have safety backs. You gotta pinch together that pin in the back before you pull them apart."

The nurse followed my instructions and her eyes widened. I don't know what surprised her more: her ability at getting off those particular earrings, or the fact I was as calm and collected enough to be able to give her the instructions as I did. I saw a nurse mouth to another and point at me: *How's she still talking?*

I felt relief being at the hospital. Much of this time I couldn't remember what was happening. I remember it was a priority for me to talk to the police about what happened since I was labeled "life or death" upon arrival. It was a flurry of doctors, nurses, specialists, interns. (It was a teaching hospital.) A couple friends sent by my oldest daughter, who was out of state, wanted to see if I was okay or not. Of course, not everyone could see me right off, not until they stabilized me. I remember doctors ordering a load of tests. I remember them saying that they thought I had left-side paralysis. There was talk of putting a plate in my skull. The doctors discussed a possible shunt. I remember getting a CT scan. In the end, they didn't do anything invasive.

I had gotten in there at about 10 pm on Wednesday evening, the first of October. The day faded into the next with plenty of interruptions. By then I had a lot of drugs in me and I don't recall which day was which, or what time it was for that matter. I do remember when my mother and my brother came. There were no flights from Minneapolis (where my family lives) to Mississippi until five the next morning. Later they told me they had stayed up all night worrying until they could get a flight out.

I remember exactly what I told them when they first saw me on Thursday morning: "I don't care that I'm paralyzed. I don't care that I'm cut up and I don't care if I'm in a wheelchair the rest of my life. I'm just happy to be alive for my kids."

My brother and my mom fell apart. We cried together.

The neurologist came in soon afterward.

"Cathy, your scalp has been shattered in so many places, we're concerned about doing surgery. It might be too dangerous and make things worse," he said.

I was in a haze. I didn't have a sense of time. I trusted the doctors in whatever they needed to do.

He talked more with my mom and brother in the hallway and I faded off again. I remember thinking before I fell into blackness: *Thank you, God, for my life, for my kids. Let me tell my story. And don't let him get away with this.*

Like I mentioned, every day in the hospital blurred into the next. I eventually stabilized. My brother Chris stayed until that next Monday, and then my other brothers Casey and Corey traveled to see me. They had to see me with their own eyes and let me know that they cared about me.

I found out my son Lincoln was safe when I saw my mom and my brother on Thursday morning. The State had put out an Amber Alert for him, and the authorities had found him. They told me that when they got to Mississippi, the authorities told them that they had Lincoln and asked them to pick him up so he wouldn't have to go into foster care. My mom told me that when they went to get Lincoln, he told them: "Daddy gave Mommy a whoopin'."

It turned out Richie had called 911. After he attacked me, he had taken Lincoln and started driving. A few minutes later, he got on the phone and called 911. His call went something like this: "You gotta go check on my wife; she's hurt bad. I hurt her. I'm the assailant." He kept using the word *assailant*, which I think is bizarre. Maybe he thought it made him more important by having a title or something. After the State put out the Amber Alert, they say he panicked and drove to a major highway, possibly to leave the state. The cops pulled him over within minutes. Then he went to the station and gave the cops a full confession.

One side of me is thankful he called and confessed; there's no doubt I would have died if he hadn't. I don't think I'm really thankful for *his* actions though. I believe it was God working through him, despite him. He wasn't really the one who called or confessed. I think God made him do it and I'm thankful to God. Richie wanted me dead. Another thing he told them is where to find the machete he used. The prosecutor now has all this evidence. They set a million-dollar bail and he's in jail awaiting trial. The authorities tell me it will be an open and shut case.

The biggest change I felt in the hospital was how grateful I was with how everything turned out. I discovered all kinds of details when I was in the hospital later that I could only attribute to the hand of God—how I called to break the window to the cop, for example. He happened to be wearing a personal body camera. The department didn't require it, and he had used his own money to buy it. He was just messing around with the camera that evening. The video that night has given me a sense of everything that happened. Without it, I don't know if I would be able to tell my story in this book. God provided for me when I needed and it's changed my life.

There were also the spooky things that happened in the attack itself that convince me God played a part in everything. Honestly, I had no idea what a machete was (the word wasn't even in my vocabulary) before I was attacked. But on the video I heard myself say it. That I put my one leg up on the loveseat, that I still have full function on my right side so I can now drive today and keep my independence, even that I was able to retain consciousness enough to tell the authorities the things I needed to say. Every example is a witness to me that God was with me, maybe even *in me* as everything happened. I even remembered exactly what Lincoln was wearing when Richie abducted him: a white T-shirt and Spiderman boxer shorts.

The work recuperating was really hard. Before, I was a middle-aged, independent mother. After, I was like a stroke patient or an old lady in a nursing home. My injuries and the paralysis gave me an excruciating schedule for physical therapy. I couldn't bathe myself. I couldn't move my left arm or leg. I couldn't even wipe myself after going to the bathroom. The nurses and therapists were angels; I'm extremely grateful for all the help they gave me. But I learned a new definition of humility in that first month in the hospital. It wasn't just the pain; the cramping afterwards made every muscle feel like a wound-up spring. My mom, who's a nurse, told me, "Cathy, this will be the most difficult task of your life. You're stubborn though, so I know you can do it." (I thank God for my stubborn streak. I think it helped me persevere with my therapy when I felt like giving up.)

During my time in the hospital, the staff kept me so busy with physical therapy and trying to heal my body that I really didn't have time to think about what had happened. I wanted to recover my physical functioning again. As hard as my physical recovery was, though, it was nothing compared to my psychological and spiritual recovery.

They released me from the hospital a little more than a month after the attack, and I moved back into my house with my mom. That's when it all came back—the attack and what led up to it. Once a week, I'd have my mom take me to Hannah, the psychologist who helped me reclaim my mind. She's also an angel from heaven and I'm thankful to God for sending her to me too. Hannah gently led me through the experience again. Every day I had to use a tape recorder and record the attack happening in real-time, second by agonizing second. They call it *prolonged exposure therapy* or *flooding*, but I like that second name because that's what it feels like at first—like the water's rushing in on you. I cried a lot and didn't want to do it after a while. Still, I made myself do it and Hannah was encouraging and kind to me. After a while, it didn't seem like I was in a closed room with water flooding in. It was more like a hose is on, but there are several exits out of the room. I have an out. Today, I'm happy to say that I don't feel like I suffer from PTSD. Richie wasn't able to take my serenity away from me.

Hannah also taught me about my thoughts, that I'm the one who owns them. She taught me that everyone has core experiences from their childhood that determine what we think about a new situation we encounter. I used to believe I was partially to blame for the abuse. No more. I catch myself thinking these negative thoughts now and I stop! And I think again. It's a new perspective to help me function in a healthy way, and recognize healthy and unhealthy relationships.

I think what makes me get up in the morning every day is the new life I've been given. I can't really explain it. You know how people who have survived near-death experiences or traumatic events say that the sky is bluer and the happiness is more intense? It sounds cheesy, but it's true. The new gratitude I've found for my life has given me a new purpose. I want to reach out to other victims of domestic violence and share my story, so something like I went through doesn't happen to them. I'm 41 years old and I've had my own husband attack me. He nearly killed me. It certainly disabled me. As much as others who see me from a distance think I look like any other middle-aged mother, it's still tough on me. I still live with physical pain from simply moving around. I don't need a walker anymore, but sometimes I still need a cane. I'm hoping that my continued physical therapy will improve my mobility and help repair my brain.

My gratitude for life also has given me a new interest in my faith. I know that when I first was saved, everything was black and white when it comes to divorce. I don't feel this way anymore. I know that God loves me. God doesn't want any woman to stay in a marriage when she's terrified to even come home. One day shortly after Richie attacked me, my mom told me that I asked to see my pastor. I do not remember asking for him, probably from all the medication I was getting or maybe because I was still recovering. I do remember what I said to him when he got there: "You have to be really careful what you tell people when you counsel them. Look at me. This is what can happen. I stayed with my abuser because of what you told me." I don't remember him responding. He didn't visit me in the hospital after that.

Plenty of other Christians did though. I still believe in the power of Jesus to change lives and move people to be better than they could on their own. My church and the people from my job did so much for my family and me when I was recuperating. They brought food of course. They put new brakes on my car for my mom. Best of all, they cleaned up the mess in my house and paid for new glass in the front door, wood flooring in the foyer, and new carpeting. God works for good in people everywhere.

When I think whether or not I would change my past if I could, I first think, *yeah … I'd change it all.* Then I remember what I have now that I wouldn't have without my attack: my son, a new gratitude that I'm even alive, and a purpose to help others. That doesn't make what Richie did right, but it does mean that God can take a horrible attack and make something good come from it. The task God has given me is to reach out to change other women's lives before it gets as bad as mine became.

I reconnected with Cathy on Facebook. I had already linked up there a year earlier with her brother Chris and his wife, Brenda, who I also knew from my high school days in marching band. I remember seeing the pleas online to help with her hospital expenses, which no doubt had grown formidable. Brenda told me that Cathy would like to work with a writer to share her story. She was particularly interested in showing what part her faith played in her recovery and how she wants to reach out to other victims of domestic violence.

Cathy lived in Mississippi until May of 2015 when she moved back to Minnesota to live with her mother in her childhood home. Although she told me she continues to have physical challenges, when I met her again, I couldn't tell that she had been in an attack. The only physical change I noticed immediately was that we had both grown older.

"But you can tell soon as I lift up my hand," she said in a Mississippi twang. She was missing the pinky on her right hand, a wound she sustained when she lifted her hand to protect herself from her attacker's rage.

"And you can see where I'm missing pieces out of my head," she said, pulling back her hair. I saw the scars the machete cut out of her skull.[7]

"But really, it ain't so bad … I'm alive. It could have been so much worse. I'm alive and that's all that matters. I'm here for my family."

Throughout the interviews, she kept repeating: "I'm just happy I'm alive," and "So many things happened that defy explanation … like how I lifted my foot up to keep my blood pressure stable, or how I told the cop it was a machete." She believes that God was not only present for her, but also that God had her do and say the things that led to her recovery.

When I asked her what spiritual virtue she believes got her through the difficulty in regaining her life she said, "That's easy. I'm grateful. Life seems different now."

I asked her in what way.

---

[7] For imagery of Cathy's injuries (trigger warning: graphic violence), please see the photo section in the center of this book.

She said, "I dunno … I don't take [life] for granted anymore. When I was lying there in a hospital bed I got to thinking—no, I was praying. I prayed 'thank you' a thousand times. God let me live. He said, 'Okay … you gotta go through this, but I'm not gonna take away everything.' I think God wants me to serve him, that I gotta get out there and tell other women in abuse situations to look at what happened to me. It could happen to them too. It doesn't have to."

Cathy believes that gratitude for her life didn't come to her until after her attack.

"I wasn't exactly a person who knew that life is precious. I mean, yeah … I'm saved and all. I know there's a God, but I didn't realize just how easy it is to lose your life. That makes what I have precious."

Gratitude and Resilience

Traumatic, life-altering events are like earthquakes that shake a city street so the newly fallen, smoldering buildings are barely recognizable. They shake apart the road you once thought you were on. Like earthquakes, you still recognize landmarks such as your relationships, or where you live, but everything is changed, your perspective skewed. You need to find a new path and you're unsure which way to go. After I had been arrested for trespassing and I sat crying, alone, in a basement jail cell, my life's trajectory was shaken. I had experienced loss and I didn't know where to turn. In these times, either we inevitably find a deeper source to orient us to a new path, or we collapse in the loss and remain in the ruins, unable to go forward.

Cathy experienced loss: the loss of mobility, the loss of a finger, and a loss of a former innocence that she could take life for granted. Like city dwellers, after an earthquake shreds apart buildings and covers the way they once knew, she needed to discover a new path. She also realized the *potential* losses she might have sustained had things gone differently. She could have been permanently paralyzed. She could have been in a wheelchair the rest of her life. She could have died. Through the losses she experienced, but also the potential losses she might have had, she came to see life through a new lens: gratitude.

Gratitude did not simply enable Cathy to resume her life, to start where she left off and continue along the same road. Instead, gratitude threw a new light on a different path, beckoning her to proceed in a new direction, together with people who cared about her.

One of the primary signs of resilience is that people are able to resume healthy relationships with others. "Of all the universal themes that have been transmitted through perennial wisdom, the expression of gratitude continues to be the glue that consistently holds society and relationships together,"[8] wrote Angeles Arrien, the recently deceased author of *Living in Gratitude: A Journey That Will Change Your Life*. Arrien believed the experience of gratitude is more than a simple feeling of thanks. Rather, gratitude is an attitude that a person decides to have. This gratitude-in-action takes practice, an effort "to take daily action that supports [a sustained] change."[9]

Gratitude is the glue that holds together the relationships Cathy cherishes. She recognizes how important her family and friends have been to her recovery. "I don't think I'd be where I am today without all the prayers and love I got those first days," she said. Her gratitude allows her to view people who care about her through a new lens, and, more importantly, respect her relationships.

---

[8] Angeles, Arrien. 2011. Living in Gratitude: A Journey That Will Change Your Life. Boulder, CO: Sounds True. 1,2.

[9] Ibid. 20, 21.

Her mother was first to notice the change in her. She said, "[Cathy] used to be pretty snotty. What I mean is that I don't think she really knew how hard it is to be a mother worrying about her daughter. From some of the things I heard before [the attack], I couldn't stop worrying about her. And I don't think I was getting the whole story on how bad the abuse had gotten …" Cathy's mother started to get emotional as she continued, "Now, it just seems like she's more open to telling me how she's feeling, what she's thinking about, what her plans for her future are. She didn't used to do this. I think we're a lot closer because of what happened. I think she's finally grateful for her mother."

Cathy's gratitude has implications that go beyond her relationships. It has given her a new attitude; she's much calmer and takes the day as it comes. That she was able to recount her harrowing story to me with barely a hint of stress was proof enough that something in her had changed. She could have taken a completely different approach to her recovery. She could have burned with anger against her abuser. She could have failed to see the wonder of simply being alive. If she had not acted out of gratitude, she would have faced the world with the same sense of entitlement and fear that she nurtured in her youth.

This observation isn't just a guess I'm making; research indicates that anger negatively correlates with resilience. A fascinating and broadly cited study published in 2003 sought to determine what role positive emotions (such as hopefulness or gratitude) had in a crisis. The researchers chose the attacks on September 11, 2001, as the crisis event. What they found was astonishing. Not only did positive emotions have a positive correlation with resilience; negative emotions *clearly* indicated a poor outcome. Anger (especially ongoing, continual anger) was the number one indicator that a person would *not* be able to resume functioning as he had before the crisis. Fuming in anger, apparently, doesn't enable us to bounce back very well.[10]

Yes, Cathy was (and still is, to some extent) angry with her abuser. Who can blame her? Her anger is appropriate and maybe even necessary. However, the anger isn't a foundation upon which she builds each new day. In my time with her, I never felt that she let anger dictate her responses. When I asked her mother what she thinks is the largest change she has seen in her daughter since her attack, her response was encouraging: "After all the horrible things ... you'd think that she'd be angry. But she's more laid back; she's grateful to be alive. Little things don't bother her like they used to." Instead, Cathy begins each day with gratitude simply for being alive. Her prayer life reflects that. She told me that offering a daily prayer for thanks is important to her; she wants to remember to be grateful. She's come through a very dark place and survived.

In our final interview, I asked Cathy what keeps her going, after the attack, now that her abuser has been arrested and is awaiting trial. Her response was telling: "God has a purpose for my life. I feel like I had to go through all I did to learn how to be grateful. Probably in a year or so I'll be doing amazing things. That's my hope at least. Here I am ... I'm 41 years old, and I needed to be almost killed to understand how I can give to other people. I'm so thankful." Gratitude enabled Cathy to let go of the anger to find serenity. Now, since she can look forward to a purpose she feels God has given to her, she doesn't have time to burn in resentment for her attacker. She looks forward to making a difference to others.

Gratitude also restores a healthy dependence on others.

---

[10] Barbara L. Fredrickson, Michele M. Tugade, Christian E. Waugh, Gregory R. LarkinW. 2003. "What Good Are Positive Emotions in Crisis? A Prospective Study of Resilience and Emotions Following the Terrorist Attacks on the United States on September 11th, 2001." *Journal of Personality and Social Psychology.* 84 (2): 365-76.

Human beings are social creatures. We depend on each other. Cathy's experience of nearly losing her life left her dependent on others. At first in the hospital, her dependence was for her physical needs. Later, she discovered that others provided for her psychological and spiritual needs in her recovery. Without gratitude, it's easy to take others' caring for granted. Worse yet, without gratitude (or with a distorted gratitude like pastors kept urging Cathy to adopt) we can develop an *unhealthy* dependence on others. This cultivates codependence and sets in motion a never-ending cycle of low self-esteem and an inability to see things as they really are. Cathy's codependence with Richie is one example of an unhealthy dependence.

The theologian and martyr Dietrich Bonhoeffer wrote about gratitude and our dependence on others during his imprisonment in a Nazi concentration camp. "In normal life, we hardly realize how much more we receive than we give, and life cannot be rich without such gratitude. It is so easy to overestimate the importance of our own achievements compared with what we owe to the help of others.[11]" Bonhoeffer's experience in prison led him to a greater understanding of what it means to be grateful, that when we recognize how much we have received from others, we begin to see our lives as a gift.

Today, Cathy is in many ways independent. However, she knows that her family and spiritual community continue to provide for her in ways she says she didn't see before. In turn, she wants to give back. She now has a purpose and a goal. She wants to reach out to other women to let them know that abusers aren't in control of their destinies or identities, that they have a choice. In this way, others can depend on Cathy as she depends on them; a healthy interdependence is what builds community, strengthening the loving bonds anyone needs.

---

[11] Bonhoeffeer, Dietrich. 2010. *Letters and Papers from Prison.* Edited by John. W. De Gruchy. Vol. 8. Minneapolis, MN: Fortress Press. 217.

Gratitude is a spiritual asset that provides the foundation for Cathy's resilience, and that asset serves as a beacon of hope she can offer others to alleviate—or prevent—their pain. Cathy's gratefulness for her life allowed her to look at life differently from the way she did before her attack. But it gave her more than just a different perspective; it gave her the hope that she might play a part in changing the horrific circumstances that some other women find themselves in. Her gratitude isn't just a tingly warm feeling to give her a positive start to the day. Instead, her gratitude, real gratitude, is a continual reminder that her very existence is a gift. Knowing it's a gift, she feels compelled to share her story and where it led her in life. She needs to pass on what she's learned to other women before it's too late for them. She chooses today to give that gift to others by being present for her family and sharing her story of how she came back stronger than she was before.

In our final interview, she said, "Since my attack, I've learned to appreciate all of the small moments in my life. I realized those moments were all I'm ever going to have." She added, "I can just sit out in the back yard and enjoy watching the wind blow in the trees, or even when Lincoln [Cathy's son] creams for my attention, it grates on me less than it used to, because, you know what? That's life." She wants others to know this gratitude through her story. "If just one woman hears my story and says, 'Yes. That's my marriage,' maybe she won't have to go through what I did. Maybe she'll know it's okay to leave because God's on her side."

A spiritual asset is a spiritual blessing or gift that allows a person to see more clearly, love more deeply, and act more courageously. As *assets*, they have a purpose for us and they make a positive difference in our lives, not only in how we function day to day but also in our ability to overcome obstacles. When we practice gratitude, we feel more at ease and we focus on the positives of that moment. Our relationships are strengthened and we learn to depend on others, just as others can depend on us.

Resilience is the ability to come back in the face of adversity or stress, and gratitude is a spiritual asset that contributes to a person's resiliency. How? It allows a person to see existence not as an enemy to defeat, but as a gift, even when bad things happen. As soon as we recognize that we have the power to control our perspective, that we can choose to see our story differently, from a place of gratitude, an unexpected gift comes to us: *hope*. This renewed perspective doesn't mean that we will no longer see difficult circumstances as the nasty things they are. Of course, no one likes to suffer. However, seeing things anew means that we have the power look at where we are right now and choose to find the potential good in any situation.

The more we find the good in difficult situations, the more we can expect to overcome the difficulties. The brighter we choose to perceive the present, even within the darkness, the more forward-leaning hope we receive from God as a byproduct. Gratitude—as a spiritual asset that undergirds resiliency—goes beyond the old cliché that "every cloud has a silver lining." Within gratitude, we come to understand that the clouds themselves may play a part in shaping who we are and who we will become. Yes, it is difficult to act out of gratitude when bad things happen. It doesn't seem to come naturally. However, we're not powerless to change our attitude to gratitude.

I've learned from Cathy's story and from my own experience that there isn't "one weird trick" we can implement and, *voilà*, we'll suddenly find the spiritual asset that will produce the resilience we yearn for through gratitude (or, for that matter, any other spiritual asset). What I can suggest is that prayer—daily, continual prayer—has the potential to change us over time. Whatever your beliefs, try it. Thank God (or whatever

Higher Power you wish) for your life, for your relationships, for breath, for the brightness of the day and for the darkness of the night. Thank God even for your suffering. Breathe in your worries and exhale your pain.

Gratitude-for-suffering isn't supposed to be an exercise in masochism or some self-flagellating ritual, wishing more ill to befall you. God doesn't want us to be miserable or to foster destructive relationships. Yet, there is some suffering over which we have no control. We can use it to teach and mold us into a new, more resilient person—even, sometimes, paradoxically through gratitude for that very suffering. A renewed prayer of gratitude for all the good things in life—people who love you, a cat meowing for her dinner, a good book whose story totally captivates you—will enable you to see the daily, the ordinary, the painful, and the disappointing in a new and more hopeful light.

Cathy has transformed her life through her resilient response to her attack. She wishes to reach out to others who have suffered so that her experience in healing may be passed along. You may contact her via email at: mysurvivalmyrebirth@gmail.com or visit her Facebook page at www.facebook.com/mysurvivalmyrebirth.

Chapter Two

Acceptance

While interviewing the people whose stories I share in the book, I don't know beforehand which spiritual asset each person will identify as foundational to their own resilience. I know only that each has a story to tell. Hunter's story immediately caught my attention, because when I pictured myself in the situations he described, I did not think I would react in the same cool-headed manner he did. Our conversation led me to ask, *what makes this guy tick?* More importantly, how does he manage to keep living without any obvious signs of PTSD?

"Hunter" is an officer in the United States Army. He has asked me to keep the details of his identity private because some of the details of his story could prove problematic for his career advancement. While nothing he said was explicitly top secret, he assured me that he wanted to be fully candid with me about his experiences. The only way he could totally open up without repercussions was to remain anonymous.

Hunter is an exceedingly likable guy. He's genuine and fun to talk with. He's articulate, and you can tell he's well educated. He speaks with a confidence that assures you he knows what he's talking about. He also conveys a deep reverence for his heritage as a Cherokee American. His ethnic background defines his response to the unavoidable stress he's endured as a soldier, and it defines the way he lives his life back at home and has a fair amount of insight into how he's changed as a result of his deployments. He has not just toned down his admittedly redneck attitudes toward people different from him; he has turned 180 degrees from the beliefs he held during his high school days.

For sure, many soldiers manage to move on with their lives after the difficult experiences of battle. Hunter has an additional protective layer to shield him from the ugliness of war. He calls it *Thinking Cherokee*, but the anthropology community calls it the *Cherokee Harmony Ethic*. The spiritual asset of *acceptance* is the best way I can think of to explain it. As he described it to me, I soon began to understand just how radically the ethic informs an understanding of life and how it completely reinterprets Hunter's response to stress, pain, trauma, and difficult circumstances.

The Cherokee Harmony Ethic isn't a matter of accepting how unfair and occasionally traumatic life is. It is decidedly not a fatalistic acceptance of injustice. Rather, it is an *active* acceptance. The Cherokee Harmony Ethic is more a recognition that each of us has little control over what happens to us, but that we do have control of our responses. Hunter's spiritual asset of acceptance undergirds the resilience he exhibits no matter what difficulties life deals him.

Hunter's Story

Sometimes a soldier has a moment in a firefight when everything slows down. It's like time decides to find a new beat, like every second begins to tick slower and slower, until even the tiniest detail comes into sharp focus. That happened to me more than once, but I'll never forget what happened in Mosul, Iraq, in 2008.

I'm a soldier with my boots on the ground. I'm the sharp end of the spear. We go where our bosses tell us to go, at any time. That means we're going in places most parents wouldn't ever want their kids straying in the daylight, much less at night. By 2008, I was a Special Operations Forces (SOF) Team Leader. I was on patrol with an infantry company when this incident took place.

That evening, my company was on patrol in a sketchy neighborhood in Mosul. I was walking down a street with my guys, clearing the streets (making sure any riff-raff wasn't lurking around the next corner to shoot us), and we were passing an alley. I was walking on the right side of the patrol, close enough to my unit but still off by myself. The Army trained us that when you pass an alleyway, you turn your weapon and point it in. You do this just in case an enemy's hiding there, waiting to shoot you. In one of those alleys stood a little, ten-year-old kid standing in the middle of it, holding a Kalashnikov, pointing the gun's barrel right at my face. He struggled with the rifle's weight; he could barely hold it, really. But there he was, aiming it at me, looking down the barrel through the gun sights. He was ready to shoot me.

I knew in that moment: *he's gonna to kill me right now.* I thought, *I'm gonna to lose my life, and I'm not gonna fire back.* Everything went through my head in a split-second. If I had the talent—I don't—I could draw that kid's face. I can see the look in his eyes even now. I can still feel his fear. I can still smell his hate. Everything had slowed down and time just stopped. The memory is embedded in my brain forever.

I am not gonna kill that kid to save my life, and I'm gonna die, right now, right here.

The kid pulled the trigger. *Click.* Nothing happened. I didn't die.

He spun around and started running away. I chased the little bastard down until I caught him. I grabbed my cultural advisor, who also was our translator. We started going door to door, trying to find that kid's family. Pretty soon, we got a tip and stood outside the kid's house. His mother came to the door and looked at him. Her face scrunched up, and she made a *pfft* sound and waved her hand behind her head. I wasn't sure if she was disgusted with him or with us being there, with him.

I instructed our unit's cultural advisor to tell the boy's mother exactly what I said and I told her the whole story as he translated. She looked at me and said, "Naam!" in Arabic, which means *yes* or *sure*. Apparently, her son's behavior didn't surprise her. But it did get her really mad.

She reached out, grabbed the boy by the collar of his shirt, and dragged him inside. As she did this, I saw the kid look back at me. His eyes are what I really remember—he was angry. If he had a functioning weapon—again—I'm sure he would have pulled it on me and tried to shoot me—again. We stood outside while his mother hauled him around the corner, inside to another room. We heard screaming and yelling. I know enough Arabic to get by, but I couldn't translate what she was shouting. But you don't need to know Arabic to understand what an angry mother might say. She was pissed. Between her sharp words, she must have been wailing on her son's tail, giving him the whooping of his life. You could hear him crying in the background. She was beating the crap out of him. After that day, incidentally, that neighborhood became a lot safer, practically overnight.

Later on, I check-fired the boy's weapon. (I had a whole stack of these guns we had confiscated.) I loaded it up and, sure enough, it fired just fine. The rest of my unit made sure to tell me: "*Holy shit, Hunter* ... you dodged one today." That kid should have killed me with that gun, but didn't. But here's the thing: I was totally fine with that. Because of the way I was raised, I was fine with it then, in the moment he could have killed me, and I'm fine with it today. I suppose I could have shot back. I could have defended myself. As a soldier, I sure would have been okay with making that choice. I didn't though, because I wasn't willing to take that kid's life in exchange for mine. I knew, right in that moment, that I was okay with dying because it meant that the boy would have gotten to live. He would have been able to grow up with the freedom to decide as a man whether to hate and kill or leave folks be.

I think this is how any of us need to live our lives, really, because the truth of the matter is that, sooner or later, we're going to leave this earth. You have to go through life like that or … you're not doing it right.

ᏎᏍᎩ, *Cherokee – (pronounced ga-du-gi): People coming together to help one another, no matter the familial connections or background of the people.*

I grew up in Oklahoma in the middle of nowhere, in the thickets, the backwoods. We did a lot of subsistence hunting. I didn't taste store-bought meat until I was in my teens. We didn't even have electricity or TV until I started seventh grade. The nearest town was fifteen miles away.

Growing up, my life was carefree. My playground was the woods in my backyard. We pumped our water up from a nearby lake. Where I lived, in eastern Oklahoma, it doesn't look like the western side of the state at all. When people think of Oklahoma, they think *plains*. Not where I'm from though—it's much hillier and wooded. It's the west side of the Ozarks really, and very green. We call it "Green Country." We lived in a little shack … actually a small trailer home. A single-wide, not those fancy double-wides they make. Everything we needed we could get from around us. We had a little garden we tended, but most of our food we gathered wild. We ate the squirrels, rabbits, and deer we killed, and we gathered the hickory nuts from the woods. One soup, *kanuchi*, I used to love. I don't get to have it as often today unless I make it myself. To make it we mashed up the nuts and formed them into balls with honey, and let it sit in a cool place for a couple weeks. When you add in hominy when it's cooking, it makes a rich and delicious soup.

My mom was a secretary and my dad worked at a local plant for a while, but I remember him recycling cans and paper for a living too. He did lots of other odd jobs as well. He even opened up a store at one time that failed miserably. Don't get me wrong, my dad passed on a sense of honor and honesty to me: he taught me what it means to be a man. He is a great guy, but he didn't have a lick of business sense and seemed to flounder from project to project. He did love the home life, though, and he cared and provided for our family at our little piece of the earth.

My Cherokee tribal citizenship comes from my mom. Historically, we've always had a matrilineal kinship system. That means a person is related only to people from her or his mother's side. I first came from my mother. I connected through her to my siblings. But, technically speaking for a Cherokee kid, I wasn't "related to" my father. My mother grew up speaking Cherokee in the home and her mother raised her in the Cherokee way. My dad can talk Cherokee too, and we switched from English to Cherokee often. The way I've described our family here is anachronistic, but today this family structure provides the basis for how we approach family. However, it has not been specifically practiced as such since the 1880s. Because of how we approached familial ties historically, our relationship toward our women is defined as one of profound respect and adoration. Clan laws were overturned in lieu of citizenship laws, but the essence of the matriarchal foundation has remained.

When I was a kid, I used to think that everyone was an American Indian. I thought that everybody all across the country had Indian blood because that's all I knew. When I finally left Oklahoma to go to college, everyone thought my belief in all people being at least part Indian of some kind was pretty strange. Now, I know better, of course. I can see how that notion would strike others as bizarre.

I had three younger brothers, but I had dozens of other younger "foster" brothers and sisters. Family is a lot more fluid with the Cherokee people than it is in most American homes. Parents traded their kids throughout the communities, depending on what the mother believed her kid should learn in life next. We always had tons of kids living with us in our own home and our family size waxed and waned. I was the eldest kid in our family. I suppose my opinions must have rubbed on some of them through the years, because when I look at some of those people today, I get a bit of a view on what I might have become, had I stayed in Oklahoma instead of gallivanting all over the world visiting five continents in the military. I also get a sense that I kept the good parts of my upbringing, like my Cherokee heritage, but that I shed other parts, like my narrow-mindedness and judgment toward others who are different from me. (I used to be quite the redneck.) I don't remember seeing a black man in real life until I was in my teens, and the only gay folks I ever met came out long after leaving the tiny piss-pot of a town I still call paradise. Bigotry was bred into me over generations of backwoods upbringing in the heart of the Cherokee Nation. I don't shun everything from my past though—I'm glad for who I am, and for who I'm continuing to become.

In Oklahoma, we don't have reservations set aside for Native communities like some other states have. We have jurisdictions. The difference is more than just semantics. The nations are semi-autonomous and we make our own decisions, though the lines between state and tribal authority can sometimes blur. Even though we're dependent on the sovereignty of the

United States, Cherokee identity will trump United States citizenship for many of the people living around where I grew up. Our identity wasn't something that we necessarily had pride in because we just took it for granted. The language, the food, the habits, the customs, the games … we *grew into* understanding the world around us through these activities.

Games like hoops, marbles, and stickball—these go back centuries and they taught us about life. The games aren't just something people do to waste time or entertain themselves with; each game has a purpose behind it to teach you an important aspect of life. Stickball especially has so many variations to its rules, depending on where and how the leaders set it up. For example, different tribes have different styles of playing stickball. Some tribes structure it with men and women both playing the game and it becomes a social event, maybe even a potential romantic one!

Stickball is the Iroquoian predecessor of lacrosse, so it's very ancient. We call stickball the "little brother of war" or *anejodi*. It taught me strategy, the importance of social connections, and toughness. It's a full-contact sport, so pain is part of the equation of course too. I suppose that game taught me to be a better soldier because pain plays a big role in that job, too. Or, I should say, pain *tries* to tell you that it's real, when it's not. You feel the pain, it's saying, "You gotta pay attention to this," but the reality is a guy can experience lots of pain and still get by. The way to ignore pain's insistent voice is to accept it, weave back into your life, and turn it into something you have to overcome. The method works.

Not all the kids in my school spoke Cherokee at home. Many of the "Country Indians" grew up talking Cherokee in everyday speech, but not very many of the "City Indians." Many of them felt ashamed of the boarding schools their parents had to attend years ago, so they didn't embrace their heritage I suppose the way I did. But you need to understand: whether or not a

Cherokee claimed his or her heritage as proudly me, that person still grew up in a culture very different from the one the rest of America experienced. I didn't realize how unique my upbringing had been until I got outside my home area later in life.

I want to make it clear that although traveling north to a white-bread college gave me a new way to look at the world (and for sure a new perspective into my own formative years growing up in rural Oklahoma), I never abandoned the way I chose to see reality. For that, I'm grateful—not just because it's made me more adaptable as a soldier within the ugliness of war, but also because I've been able to appreciate adversity as something that enriches life. Pain, suffering, hardship can be a gift. That doesn't mean I seek it out. I'm not a masochist. It's more like I feel an appreciation for adversity as an inevitable part of what it means to be human. Adversity provides me a place to weave my values back into the world to make our community—local to global—better. Maybe that's one reason woven things like baskets or textiles are considered sacred to Cherokees. They are a metaphor for how we treat adversity—we weave it into who we are instead of trying to throw it away or actively avoid it.

For as much as I now know my coming of age was unique, part of my growing up you will recognize as typically American. I still went to an American high school in the heart of the Midwest. I played sports and went to prom. I watched movies and I learned to drive a car. Sometimes I ate burgers and I went to keggers. I'm an American and seem phenotypically white (I look like a white guy), but my heart is Cherokee. My response to the world is uniquely Cherokee. Call it a lens through which I interpret everything, or maybe it's more like a pair of eyeglasses I can't ever take off—I act according to what we call *thinking Cherokee*, and that way of seeing the world is very different from the way most Americans were raised to react to life.

When I turned eighteen, I had to make a decision about what

I would do as an adult. Again, the ways we go about making a big decision is different from the way most other American kids probably go about it.

According to old clan identity, when a kid becomes an adult in the Paint Clan he or she is encouraged to either teach, go into medicine, or to become a warrior—all very respected professions. I had a queasy stomach, so becoming a doctor or nurse was out. I knew I didn't have the patience to be a teacher. It looked like I was supposed to become a warrior. The matriarch holds the decision-making in a family or clan sub-group, and from what she says, the family follows. So I had to get permission from my grandmother to learn to be a warrior.

There's another aspect of our life I want you to understand. Cherokees come together and help each other, and this way of life influences our concept of—and response to—stress and pain. It's a concept we call *gadugi*. Gadugi is the community ethic to naturally help a person, no matter where they come from or who they are. Some outsiders see it as simply community or community building, but it's much more than that. At its core, gadugi is a centering of wills and minds to accomplish a communal task. Historically, these tasks would have been working together at harvest time or raising a home. Gadugi as a concept has grown to encompass the enmeshing of individual thoughts and desires to accomplish something that needs doing, collectively, despite the hardships everyone needs to overcome.

I look to my own decision to become a warrior as an example of gadugi. At the point my grandmother gave me her blessing to become a warrior (which my father was firmly against), it was cemented in everybody's minds that they were going to help me become that. Straight out of high school, I joined the National Guard. I became an infantryman. After training, my grandmother decided it would be good that I get an education. Everyone agreed and my family did everything they could to help me achieve that goal with both financial and moral support. I ended up going north—way north—to study at a little college and apply for ROTC training. The choice to travel far away from my home to study shocked my family at first. People raised in my community don't usually decide to leave the area, much less the state. But grandmother was for it, so off I went. And my family supported me in that decision because that's what we do—we help each other to achieve a shared goal.

Incidentally, the Cherokee Nation tribal government has decided recently to embrace and promote the concept of gadugi. The *GaDuGi Health Center* is a clinic in Tahlequah, Oklahoma, the capital of the Cherokee Nation. And others are beginning to catch on to the idea too—the rape crisis center in Lawrence, Kansas named their organization the *Gadugi Safe Center*. It's good that the idea is spreading, but I do hope they strive to communicate the nuances of the word, that it's not just a translation for "community," but rather is an active approach to form bonds and support the work both individuals and groups of people do. Gadugi is about reinforcing the common good, whether it's for a whole community or just one person.

After I traveled north, I finished college in the spring of '95. I got my degree in International Relations and the ROTC training I was after. But my destiny to become a warrior would have to wait, mostly because I was about to become a father.

I met my girlfriend, believe it or not, fundraising for the Republican Party. (If anyone met me now, they'd be surprised to learn I did this because after having seen the world, my political leanings became much more progressive.) My girlfriend was the crazy punk-rock girl, and neither us were very good Republicans, although we managed to raise money for the cause and hang out with each other. I liked her because she was wild and opinionated, like me. In the beginning, the relationship had been a friendship and purely platonic. One night she and I both had a little too much to drink, and one thing led to another. It was an accidental thing as many things are when you're young and dumb. Then all of the sudden, I had a daughter. Being a new dad isn't especially conducive to high-tailing it away with the military. Since I wanted the best for my new kid and my girlfriend (who soon after became my first wife), I elected to stay home for a bit. I informed the military of my situation and we decided it would be best for us to move back to Oklahoma, closer to family.

We packed up our belongings as best they would fit into a trailer attached to the dinky blue Geo Prism my grandmother had helped me buy. We were all set to move back to home. There was only one problem. Before we could leave, I realized that I didn't have enough gas money to get home. There we were, stranded in North Dakota with a dog, our Geo Prism, and a trailer in tow, with not a lot of choices.

I had collected coins ever since I was a kid and I had managed to string together a fairly significant (and valuable) rare coin collection. At a truck stop, I managed to make a connection with someone who might be interested in my collection. I brought the coins to him and he offered me two hundred and nineteen bucks for the whole thing. Some of the coins I knew were worth thousands—two, in particular, had significant value. I told the guy that he could have it all except for those two.

He said, "No. Two-hundred-nineteen for the whole thing, or you can go fuck yourself." He had me over a barrel and we had no other options. I sold the coins.

I don't fault the guy for it though. At least, I hope the coins put his kids through college after he sold them for the profit I'm sure he knew he'd get. (That's the story he fed me, anyway, that he was raising money for his kids.) The way I look at it is that life's just like that: it's painful, and sometimes you get screwed. I could choose to stick it to other people when I have the upper hand too, but I don't because that's not the way the mothers raised me. And sure, I don't go out looking for situations where people can take advantage of me, but when they do—like with selling my coins to that guy—I don't let it eat at me. Instead, I weave the experience into the fabric of my story, my life.

We lived in Oklahoma for a while and my wife and I had another child. I worked odd jobs and continued to fulfill my commitment with the National Guard when I could. In about '98 we moved to Texas and things took a turn for the worse. My wife was ... unstable. She had struggled with mental health issues and some drug abuse in the past, but our relationship turned sour and she didn't take care of our kids like I thought we both should have done. By '99, she had moved out and I had become a single dad. We divorced in '01. By 2002, I had met another woman, whom I would eventually marry and stay married to.

Fast forward to late 2002. I had received orders to go to Iraq; my National Guard unit was activated. My ex showed up, literally hours before I was supposed to be deployed. The plan had been for her to pick up the kids, and care for them temporarily while I served in combat. However, she showed up with paperwork and fiancée in tow. I had to either sign the legal documents that stated she would be the permanent legal guardian, or she wasn't going to take the kids. My girlfriend couldn't legally take them, so my choice was either sign over the kids to my ex and not know if I'd ever see them again, or I could refuse and I would have had to go AWOL and end up in jail. It was too late to find alternate care among my family. I was a lieutenant at the time, and I was in charge of a platoon, so the legal and ethical ramifications for abandoning my unit would have been disastrous, both for me, but also for my kids. Again, someone had me over a barrel. I signed the paperwork.

I'll be honest—it bothered me. On the journey over, I thought about my kids a lot. I wondered whether my ex was going to treat them well. I wondered if she was going to be stable enough and not use drugs around them. But I finally came to believe that I could either let something like this eat at me, or I could weave the frustration, the worry, and the pain into my life. I decided the latter because that's what I do. It's the Cherokee way. I wasn't stuffing all the pain away; I made it a part of who I was. I'm glad I did that because I wouldn't have been able to focus on my role as a warrior, a soldier, if I had just fussed about it. I had to actively accept my ex's decision, and just live with it.

Our first tour landed us in Egypt to enforce the Camp David Accords. Then we crossed the berm through Kuwait and came up to Basra. The war in those early years was a bit like the Wild West. The Command gave us basically coffee cans filled with money and we bought vehicles from the locals. We called them bongo trucks (not the Kia model). In those days, many units across the military were under-supplied. Since we were infantry, most of this first tour was either communicating with the locals, many of them Bedouins, to find out what the enemy was doing, or we were shooting the occasional firefights that came up. It was stressful, but like any battle-hardened soldier, I managed. Some didn't though.

The stress got to one kid in our group. (I referred to all my guys as kids.) About a year after our deployment, this kid blew his brains out. Thinking back on it, I think it was that he had felt like he had been a burden on the rest of our team and no way to redeem himself after the fighting was over. It was hard on our unit because during that deployment we hadn't lost any of our guys to the enemy. It was hard on me too. Don't think that the Harmony Ethic means that you don't feel the massive weight of losing a kid who thought he wasn't part of us, that he was a burden to us and had to take his own life. Losing that kid was like losing one of my own. But the way I dealt with it was the same I had done in the past: I wove it into who I was.

Ironically, the way I functioned and managed was exactly the opposite of what the military had taught me. The military teaches you to compartmentalize. It's pretty much the opposite of Harmony Ethic. The Army teaches you to pack trauma and stress away until you can deal with them later. The way we grow up as Natives is that we take that pain and weave it into our lives. We welcome the pain in, because there's nothing you can do to change it, and by its very existence, the pain has already changed you. We take the pain in, because there is no way you can really compartmentalize or segregate that pain. You have to create the harmony of the good and the bad and say to yourself: *the good and the bad come together. The bad stuff happened, it did, but it doesn't destroy who I am at my core.*

After the first tour, I traveled back home. The situation with my kids didn't turn out as bad as I had thought. My ex grew tired of taking care of our kids, and despite any paper I signed, she decided that partying and coming home late was much more fun than holding down a steady job and making macaroni and cheese for the kiddos. I got my kids back. I married another gal and I worked in corporate America until I was deployed. Again.

For the following deployments, the military decided that it was much better to sufficiently equip us. For one, we didn't need to purchase those bongo trucks to get around with any longer, but we had other provisions like decent med kits and clothing too. From then on, fighting was much less the improvised, get-what-you-can-and-go than it had been the first time. By then, I had been promoted to Captain. My job was to be around the population—our unit's job required that we influence the local people. Sometimes that meant we'd pay folks to get information. Other times it meant that we'd have to fight or at least pressure people to get them to do what we wanted them to do. Sometimes, we discovered who the bad guys were, and we'd have to chase them down and kill them, if necessary. We did our best to leave that to the grunts, though.

I loved the infantry as a place of punctuated and slightly choreographed violence, structured to give merit and focus to anger with an emotional staccato any young Okie Officer could really sink his teeth into. We were all men, mostly white, homophobic, red-blooded Americans itching for a fight. It was the work for which I was made. I could shoot, move, and communicate, parachute from airplanes, and endure austerity, the likes of which other more refined individuals write novels about. I was that invincible jackass the government pays good taxpayer money to ensure gasoline stays cheap, America remains #1, and that people across the globe know their "rightful" place.

Eventually, I left the infantry for a part of the Army's Special Operations Forces (ARSOF) and I excelled there, as well. No longer would I be expected to kill enemies of the state and break their stuff as the primary objective. Death and destruction would need a specific purpose, and life would be preferred until such time as the enemy's demise made more sense strategically. Often as a commanding officer, I was the one who got to decide life or death.

Sometime after the kid had tried to off me from that alleyway in Mosul when his gun jammed, I found myself again in Mosul, just after the so-called surge, when massive increases in troop levels drove the radicals from Baghdad elsewhere. Unfortunately for me, "elsewhere" happened to be Mosul, which up to that point had been pretty peaceful, as war zones go. My job often had me working with small teams amongst the population and I got to know people at a less threatening level—except when they tried to kill me. That wasn't all the time, but it did happen at least once a day.

One day, I was out with an adjacent unit following up with

the goings on of a suicide-vest cell, when the world exploded just a mile away. And, although we're clearly not as brave as Marines on recruiting ads are, we ran toward the explosion with reckless abandon. Nothing ... *nothing* during my previous fifteen years of service could've prepared me for what we found. Later, the media called it "the Mosul Hiroshima."

An Iraqi EOD (Explosive Ordnance Disposal) unit had been trying to disarm an HBIED (House-Borne Improvised Explosive Device). Some creative individual or group had decided to turn a whole building into a bomb. Unfortunately, the Iraqi unit assigned to disarm the bomb neglected to search the whole building. They didn't realize that there was an explosives and weapons cache in the sub-basement of the structure. So they decided to detonate only the bombs they could see on the first floor, the ground level. Their mistake ended up igniting everything. The resulting blast leveled not just the house, but a neighborhood full of families as well. My boys and I went there to help pick up the pieces.

I spent three sleepless days picking up those pieces ... *literal pieces* of people's lives. It now haunts me. One quirk of human psychology has to do with conditioning, and conditioned nobility has a way of making itself known in unexpected ways. For me, protecting others became a blind habit. So, over the years, up to this time in my life, I had been constantly conditioned to protect those who could not protect themselves, and the face of carnage was never too far away. Up to that point, I'd seen the "other"—those who couldn't protect themselves—as exactly that: *not me—not my people.* (Of course, the knuckleheads we shot at qualified as the "other" too.)

But this was different. It changed me because weaving that carnage into my life's experience displaced something. The death I saw no longer bore nationality nor melanin content nor politics nor sexual orientation. They were just people. Dead people. People who once had been someone's sister, brother, wife, child, friend. Something cold and taut inside me loosened at some point. I don't remember the exact moment, but I remember the slackening of a displaced center. My center, my core, my anchor-of-certainty measuring my own worth against the differences I saw in others had shifted. The redneck identity that brought me through years of combat had changed, and I was embarrassed of the man I'd been, only days before.

Something else happened—I was proud of the heritage my grandmother had taught me in a new way. Harmony, I realized, wasn't just about me or how I defined myself against "other" people. Picking up those pieces had taught me something new. I saw that maybe *gadugi* was a community more expansive than I had realized. I thought, *maybe community is everyone*, and the delineations we impose are really artificial. Sure, as a soldier—a warrior—I need to defend those who can't do so themselves. Sometimes that means I take out the knuckleheads shooting at me. But more often it means that I stop and listen, try to learn and feel the pain others are feeling—even if that means I need to weave some of their pain into myself.

Looking back now on the redneck I was, full of hatred that I hadn't recognized as such, I sometimes feel pity for the man I was, as if I should weep for his ignorance of the fragility and preciousness of life. It's easy for most folks born of upper-middle class ideals to suspend natural suspicions of the "other," because their place in the world feels secure. But that ability is tenuous; they've usually not earned it. Those of us who have truly seen the darkness know all the more what the light is. Or at least what it ought to be.

A person earns perspective, maybe wisdom too. Although I still exist in the shadows of many things—my past and the horrible memories I have to continue to weave into my life, even now. I can finally see light. I no longer have the capacity to care about your skin color, whether or not you can make babies, with whom you share your bed, or where you were born. I've seen true ugliness; it's made me learn to accept others as they are, and not as I think they should be. This has been the greatest discovery of my life. I know it's made me a better person. Maybe it's given the ability to face a new day too, because whatever happens in the future, good or bad, joy or stress, I know that my role as a warrior ultimately is to fight for the well-being of all people, no matter where they come from or what they believe.

I spoke with Hunter on three separate occasions, each for about an hour to an hour and a half. He shared a few other typical war stories with me—guys shooting at each other, an incident when a suicide-vest commander (I discovered the people we call suicide bombers actually have bosses—none of whom feel the need to martyr themselves) triggered a vest on the victim too early, and a few others detailing the *psyop* his special unit engaged in. He asked that I keep some of those out of the story to protect his identity. The stories weren't what I was really interested in, anyway. I wanted to know what the weaving process he referred to meant.

I wondered how a person goes about implementing Cherokee Harmony Ethic. I wanted to know how it "works." At first, it seemed he avoided my question. However, Hunter likes to tell stories. He's also a thinker, and he wants you to know the reasons why "thinking Cherokee" is hard for people of European descent to understand. I asked him directly how the Harmony Ethic is different from the way other people deal with pain and stress.

He said, "A lot of people are brought up thinking that everything is gonna be okay, that [they] deserve good things to come from life. I mean ... who doesn't want this? It's the American way! But thinking Cherokee is really the opposite of that. Life isn't about what you can get out of it." His answer surprised me; I think that most, if not all, people have life goals and want to get something back.

Asking him to explain more, he said, "[Life] is what you can *put back into it* from what you have inside. When you don't try to shield yourself against all the bad experiences life has to offer—divorce, addictions, war … you name it—you can weave who *you* are back into the world and make it a better, stronger fabric."

I asked him if he regretted seeing the horrific explosions or experiencing bloody, life-or-death combat.

"No. Not at all! That's what I'm saying—a guy doesn't have to go out and seek to find the bad junk. No. That's part of life—the hard times will come on their own. Probably as a soldier I've seen lots more [violence] than you have. But the point I'm trying to make is that I don't want to shield myself from any of it. It doesn't matter if it's a messy divorce, or when some knucklehead in Afghanistan detonates a vest prematurely on a guy they conned into being a martyr. When these nasty things happen—or anything else—I don't run away. I weave them into who I am, so I can then weave myself back into the world for the good I can do."

"Harmony Ethic isn't about finding balance, because balance provides a net movement in life of *zero*. It's not taking something good *against* something bad; it's about taking all the experiences as they come and finding a place for them, within you."

I shared with Hunter my own understanding of acceptance within Twelve Step recovery, and how it relates to my life in recovery from addiction. I wanted to make a connection with his insight into the weaving process, and especially how it makes him more resilient. His response gave me a new way to look at acceptance—that maybe it was something much deeper than I had thought.

"Acceptance [by itself] is passive. Harmony Ethic is active. Stress, trauma, loss, pain … these aren't my enemies. No. I think they're my friends! Whether weaving a fabric, a basket, or a song, they all provide us the sacred model of harmony. It's learning to sing your own song. Sometimes that song has the painful lines, other times it's got the joyful, fun-loving lyrics. But your song is *your* song. You can't separate the bad from the good. I suppose you could call it *active* acceptance. But the term I use isn't something I've really thought about. Up to now, before talking with you about it all, I would have just called it *thinking Cherokee*.

"For us, we take it one step further than passive acceptance. For us, we weave the bad in with the good, so that we can create a harmonious chord as a response to the dissonance of the world, and all the misery that goes with it."

I asked Hunter how he defines harmony.

He said, "I think it has to do with the attitude that how the world affects not only you—you're just *a part* of this world, a larger community. What you do matters! It's our duty to make the world a better place. That's harmony. You take whatever the world gives you. You make it a part of you. You make the fabric of the world stronger. You weave your own song back into that of the world"

The metaphor of fabric fascinated me. I asked, "Why fabric? Is it possible that fabric doesn't explain why there is evil in the world to begin with?"

Somewhat irritated with my lack of understanding, he replied, "Look, this isn't difficult. Fabric—or any woven material or melodic chord—holds itself together by binding itself to the other strands of thread or notes around it. We're exactly the same. The more we see that life isn't about an individualistic challenge to conquer or overcome, and the more we see that, instead, we're in this together, for better or worse, the more we will recognize we need to accept whatever we're dealt. That's not a promise that everything will work out in the end. For lots of folks, it doesn't. I've seen that firsthand. What it means for me is that my experiences—bad or good—aren't the end of it all anyway. The Creator weaves the fabric of life for a purpose greater than any of us really knows. I'm just happy to be a thread, a simple part of something much larger."

I finally understood. Cherokee Harmony Ethic was not so much a systematic theology seeking to cover every doctrinal possibility, but instead a story through which to reinterpret the world around us. To Hunter, his understanding of the world as a place that naturally gives us experiences—both good and bad—is a gift. Period. For him, how he chooses to take the gifts and weave them back into his life I believe makes him a more resilient person.

Acceptance and Resilience

A spiritual asset is a spiritual blessing or gift that allows a person to see more clearly, love more deeply and act more courageously. As *assets*, they make a positive *difference* in our lives, not only in how we function day to day, but also in our ability to overcome obstacles. When we practice acceptance (and *active* acceptance in the way that Hunter described the Cherokee Harmony Ethic), we find that the external circumstances that we perceive as uncomfortable—or even unbearable—don't have to control our responses. Acceptance is more than resignation. That would be just giving up or acquiescing. Instead, *active* acceptance is first acknowledging the pain, then courageously turning toward it and weaving it back into the world. I believe this is what Hunter was trying to tell me, but I didn't at first quite get, because I kept returning to my understanding that acceptance means we don't let that "bad stuff" bother us so much. That's not what he was saying at all. In fact, he shared that what he's seen and done *did* bother him, and seeing people's body parts strewn on a street in war-torn Iraq still continues to haunt him. The difference with him is that he sees that experience as something vital to his identity.

Resilience is the ability to come back in the face of adversity or stress, and acceptance is a spiritual asset that contributes to a person's resiliency because it allows a person to see existence not as an enemy to defeat, but as a gift, even when bad things invariably happen. Hunter's story taught me that we have the power to control our perspective—that we can choose to see our story differently, from a place of acceptance where we can embrace life's difficulties and purposefully claim them as part of who we are and use them to help others.

As I spoke with Hunter, I became aware of his frustration in explaining the Harmony Ethic to me, especially in light of what he's endured as a soldier. I got the feeling that his upbringing ingrained this Ethic so deeply in him that he had difficulty articulating it. I could relate to the frustration. Often when I'm describing addiction to a person who hasn't gone through it themselves (or who doesn't at least have a friend or a relative who has suffered from it), I sense a profound disconnect with them. I feel as if I'm speaking another language. I've learned that I need to find commonalities if I'm going to convey more than information, to communicate the struggles—and just what overcoming those struggles entails.

Maybe Hunter sensed my frustration. I kept coming back to the question: *how do you do it?* The more we talked, though, I came to understand that his "active acceptance" of the frustrations, the pains, the stresses, the anguishes, and the terrors he's witnessed weren't about specific actions he takes. It's a complete attitude shift toward life itself. At its core, the Harmony Ethic is looking at life differently from the way many of us from a European heritage naturally do. It's a completely different worldview, defined by a culture much removed from that of mainstream America, though one that lives still vibrantly alongside it.

An example for you: I love planning for vacations. I think I like planning for them (and dreaming about them) almost more than I do taking them. Last year, my mother suggested that my family accompany her on a trip to Alaska. I'd never been to Alaska before and my mother is getting older. She was footing the bill and we were all going to go first class. Whitewater rafting, fishing, a special trip on a small plane from Denali … all of that stuff we were going to do together. It was going to be a real adventure, a family expedition.

When we got to Alaska, things were going swimmingly. Until about three days into the trip, when I read the waiver we had to sign to go on the small plane trip. There is nothing like a legal document to scare the living crap out of you what *could* go wrong, and this waiver had it all spelled out, of course, to protect the outfitters against any liability they *might* have in the case of our untimely demise.

Added to the fact that I'm naturally a histrionic who over-reacts, I began to think twice about the small plane ride from Denali to Anchorage. I even got on my phone and started to look on the Internet for the statistics about plane crashes in Alaska. I shared the information with my ten-year-old son, Nathan, who wondered what I was reading next to him on the bus seat. By the time the tour guide came around to collect the waiver forms from us, Nathan was crying in his seat. He said he didn't want to die. Then, I doubled down with my mother and my wife and made everything worse. We ended up skipping the plane trip and instead took the bus ride back to Anchorage.

Looking back on my decision, I see how stupid I was. At the time I thought I was making an informed decision for the safety of my family. (And probably the drama of the situation stimulated my brain.) The point I'm making is that I came from a generally unrecognized, but wholly sanctioned American standpoint that,

(1) Life is inherently dangerous.

(2) We should do everything possible to prevent bad stuff from happening, so we can protect what we already have.

With the Cherokee Harmony Ethic, Hunter approaches the world quite differently. From what he told me, it seems he comes from the standpoint that,

(1) Life is inherently dangerous.,

(2) I should not actively seek out bad things from happening.

(3) When I do encounter difficulties, I will accept them, and more than that, I will grab ahold of them as a gift to weave compassion back into the world.

The Cherokee Harmony Ethic *accepts life on life's terms*, not "accepting life on *my* terms," which has become the post-modern mantra that we can make our own reality.

The reading I've done on this topic seems to affirm Hunter's description of the values he was taught in his upbringing, that true harmony is about actively accepting the situations you find yourself in life. Here is an excerpt from *The "Harmony Ethic" of the Conservative Eastern Cherokees: A Religious Interpretation by John D. Loftin, the* widely-acclaimed author of Native American spiritual practices in the United States:

> Cherokees understand themselves more as "being oriented" than as "becoming oriented." That is to say, they feel that the world constitutes them more

than they constitute the world. [They] do not
attempt to "better themselves" through ambitious,
future-oriented self-assertion. To be a [Chero-
kee] means to take one's proper place among that
which is already the case, to follow the path set
before one. Hence, the Cherokee attempt to come
to terms with the world they perceive ... and in
so doing they seek to be, not "better," but as they
were in the Beginning.[12]

What Loftin describes here is not an acquiescence to accept
one's lot in life, no matter what social inequalities exist. Cherokee Harmony Ethic isn't so much about bending to social
injustices. Instead, this ethic of active acceptance is more like
allowing everything that can happen, to simply happen—to
allow the bad and the good to flow over us like water over a
stone in a streambed. Though part of the river, and subjected to
its power, the stone is not only changed by the river over time
but is itself able to change its tiny part of the river, bending
it in a new way, weaving the waters through and around its
presence without corrupting the river's course.

The closer I listened to Hunter, the more I began to see that
active acceptance/Harmony Ethic is ultimately about affirming
the community over the individual. It would seem that the
Cherokee concept of *gadugi* fits well within a larger framework
of how the Cherokee people see themselves not as individuals
disconnected from the whole, but part of the whole itself.

Still, I wanted to make the connection between all the different
concepts I had learned—gadugi, harmony, active acceptance—
with Hunter's spirituality. More importantly, how does his ethic

---

[12] Loftin, John D. "The "Harmony Ethic" of the Conservative Eastern
Cherokees: A Religious Interpretation" *Journal of Cherokee Studies*. vol. 8,
no. 1. 139.

contribute to his resilience? To get at this question, I asked him point blank how he defines harmony. His answer was telling.

After a long pause, he said, "It helps me to think of our idea of harmony as one of our baskets, or tapestries, or blankets, or songs. All woven things are sacred models to us. We're each of us both thread and weaver. Life, existence is the whole. We take what's around us and weave ourselves into the whole, no matter what that looks like, because in the whole, there is strength to abide the weaker points in each individual thread. We find our place and take our pain with us to add that richness to our tribe and into our person. Pain is … a beautiful gift that helps to create our place in the universe. That's harmony—it's just finding our place in a tune … or as a thread in the bigger basket. And it's something you continue to discover. Finding my place will never end."

I wondered if harmony was finding a balance to our lives.

"No. Balance and harmony to us are opposites. Balance is inherently without motion and life can't endure stillness for long. So, with things like justice which are symbolized by balance scales, we usually see far more value in finding a way forward by "weaving" offenders back into the tribe than punishing guilty parties. Forgiveness is more valuable to the tapestry, when possible, even when it's painful. Perhaps especially so. The only exceptions I can think of are when a thread is intentionally cut with murder or an elder or child is abused (both of which harm the whole) and then … accountability is necessary to maintain the harmony, but even then, it's only to set conditions for forgiveness."

Acceptance from a western, modern point of view is passive. Hunter's understanding of the Cherokee Harmony Ethic redefines acceptance as an active choice, a new way to see the world. He showed me that anyone has another option than simply shrugging off stress and trauma as an inexorable consequence of life. He taught me that our perception of stress, trauma—even terror—matters. What's more is that the Harmony Ethic doesn't downplay or diminish the heartache or pain. Instead, this active acceptance transfigures the pain into a useful tool for compassion. I am personally thankful that I came to understand Hunter's story; it makes sense in light of all that happened to me (and because of my actions) in North Dakota. I now see that the more I have been willing to accept, to own, *and to embrace* my story of addiction and redemption, the more resilient I am to whatever life throws at me, good or bad.

Chapter Three

Hope

In March of 2011, I was a patient at Hazelden's treatment facility in Center City, Minnesota, when the Arab Spring movement began to spread from Tunisia to Libya. At that time, Hazelden wasn't allowing patients to access the Internet, so I got my news the old-fashioned way from a newspaper. I read several stories about the uprisings and became fascinated with the intricate maps the AP provided of the war's progression in Libya. I've always been interested in international politics and during my time in rehab the news was a welcome distraction from the painful transformation I was going through. I remember feeling excited about the possibility that the world was changing for good. It seemed the dictators would finally get their due. Democracy would win.

What I didn't know was how difficult and painful a transformation it would become for the people living in those countries. (And as things have turned out, at least so far, the uprising hasn't led to positive transformation but to unbelievable disaster.) Also, each country had its own particular complications as their respective revolutions unfolded. I had no idea that Syria would be a country that would soon fall into disarray. In fact, I didn't know anything about Syria; much less personally know anyone from there.

The past year, I connected with a Greek man who made

an online video I viewed, showing his work with an organization helping Syrian refugees. I thought a refugee's story would
exemplify stress and trauma and would prove valuable in this
book. No one flees their homeland unless they're forced out
under great duress. Also, a story from a refugee's perspective
is timely, because politicians have made a football out of the
question of whether refugees are a terror threat in the United
States. I reached out to him and he responded, and provided
me with a contact I could interview.

Through my Greek connection, I met Raja (*RAH-jah*, not his
real name). The name is Arabic for "hope" and he requested I
use this name when referring to him.[13]. He shared with me his
incredibly heartbreaking, but hopeful, story. He requested not
only that I change his name to signify hope, but also change
the places and other details of his story because there are still
factions in Syria (mostly foreign opposition) who might seek
vengeance against his friends and relatives still living there if
they were to discover his story had been published.

My interview with Raja was a complicated ordeal. I don't
speak Arabic, and his English is quite broken. What's more is
that I discovered that Google Translate is exceedingly poor at
translating Arabic into English. I assumed Raja had a similar
experience when I sent him my questions in English. Not
surprisingly, we became frustrated with our inability to understand one another via Skype and email. I finally acquired the
services of a translator, which made our conversation all the
more time-consuming, but worthwhile in the end.

What's most compelling about his story are the moments
when we sense that Raja could lose all hope. I wondered several
times if I would have given up, had I been in the same situations. However, hope—not a fleeting desire, but a persistent

---

[13] Interestingly, both men and women can have this name; a person's
gender is determined by how it's pronounced.

belief that something good may yet come—is a powerful motivator. The distress and horror of the Syrian civil war became the crucible in which Raja's hope was forged. His hope is not a wish or yearning that his circumstances will one day improve. Instead, he *already believes* that one day, his circumstances will be better. Raja's hope is the reason to keep going through the night, even when the dawn seems like it might never come.

Raja's Story

I was born and raised in the city of Homs located in west-central Syria, just to the northeast of Lebanon. Homs *was* a beautiful city. I hope people will one day rebuild it to its former splendor, but I do not see that happening anytime soon. The city was dubbed the "mother of the poor," because people there reached out to help one another, and the cost of living was cheaper than the larger Syrian cities of Aleppo and Damascus. The cultural heritage of Homs was also one of its important features. Its history runs deep—the city was settled over two thousand years before the birth of Jesus.

The majority of the once beautiful and stately buildings have since been reduced to rubble. A nearby UNESCO World Heritage site, *Krak des Chevaliers* (a citadel from the time of the Crusaders), today sits in ruins. It is sad to see people destroy history—it's all we have to remind us of our shared past. The strife in our country has not only destroyed our cultural heritage but has also ruined millions of lives. Nearly every home is riddled with bullet holes or crumbling walls. The Syrian civil war has robbed me of many things, even people whom I loved. Still, the toll the war has taken, there remains one blessing I hold closely. No amount of violence or cruel terror can take away this precious treasure—my hope.

Palestinian poet Mahmoud Darwish wrote, "And I tell myself, a moon will rise from my darkness."[14] My hope is that my story will become a rising moon for my people and my family to radiate the truth of what has happened, that so many who have died will be known, and our suffering will be known. I hope that by reading my story, you will come to understand what hardship the Syrian people have gone through. The world doesn't know our struggles. Or if people do know, they seem to have ignored our cries for help. Only when people know and change their governments' policies of throwing us away, will my hope become realized.

Before our family transitioned into mainstream Syrian society, I lived in a Palestinian refugee camp, within the city limits of Homs. I come from a Palestinian family who suffered because it was deprived of its homeland. My father was among the people whom Israel forced out of Palestine in 1948 when he was only a few months old. During that period, the Palestinians were refuged in Syria, Lebanon, and Jordan. My father and mother landed in a refugee camp in Syria several kilometers from the center of Homs, and I was born into that world. Our refugee camp was under the supervision of the United Nations, an organization that provided us with health and educational services. I attended a school in a rickety UN building until I was seven. By the mid-1980s, our family had transitioned from the refugee camp into the mainstream society. Today, I am Palestinian, but also Syrian. It is my home after all.

My father suffered because of the harsh living conditions

---

[14] Darwish, M. (2013). Innan's Milk. In M. Darwish & A. El-Zein (Ed.) Translated by M.A. Forche, *Unfortunately, It Was Paradise.* Berkeley, CA: University of California Press. 100.

in the refugee camps and the difficulty of raising us. We often had very little to eat, and my siblings and I got sick a lot. I was one of seven sons and his concern was to educate us so that we might inherit a brighter future. He did his best, even though his salary was sufficient for only the first half of the month. The second half, we barely managed to scrape by. My father worked every day and most nights to provide for his growing family's needs. He worked so hard because my brothers and I meant everything to him. We were his hope and dream because he knew he could no longer live for his own aspirations, his desire since childhood to become a rich and successful businessman. He accepted his lot in life as a common worker so that he might give us a promising future.

My father died when I was still in high school. It was a shock to me. I still remember the last words he had said to me, "Where were you? Why are you so late? We were waiting for you to have dinner!" Like most guys my age, I was interested in things other than being on time for a family dinner. As a sat down at the table that night, I burned with resentment against my father's chiding the way only a teenager can, like a flame you see from a roadside warning flare. Little did I know that meal would be the final one with all of us still together. The next day when I was getting ready for school, my father had a heart attack. He died in front of me and I was helpless to save him. I regret my actions at our last meal together, but I cannot change the past. Today I know that the times I spent with my father were some of the happiest days of my life. I miss him dearly.

After my father died, our mother had to play the roles of both parents. She became our provider and comforter. Since her time was stretched so thin, I think she was on the verge of emotional collapse. So my older brother and I decided to quit school and started working to compensate for our family's shortage of income. At the time, I was in the eleventh grade. It

66

was 1994. My older brother and I started working in odd jobs to make ends meet until my siblings had a chance to grow up. Most of them went on to study in the university or received professional training.

I joined the mandatory service in the Syrian National Army in 1996 and finished my military duty by '99. It was a difficult period, but with the help of God and my mother's efforts, I finished my studies and began working as a painter and decorator of homes. In 2001, when I was 27, I got engaged to my high school sweetheart. Our love for each other seemed to reignite out of thin air. I hadn't spoken with her much since my school days, but the love between us apparently never had completely burned out. My relationship with "Khalila"[15] became the happiest event for me since my father had died. I started down this path optimistic, hopeful that things would work out for us. Soon after marrying, our family had grown; God had graced us with a boy, then a girl. I pledged to myself that I would provide them with all the things I had been deprived of. Given my work as an interior decorator, we lived as comfortable a life as we could manage, but the truth was that we were poor. Dirt poor. Whatever I could spare from my monthly earnings I passed along to my mother and siblings who still needed the financial support.

Even though we were poor, we were happy. Do you know how poor people live in happiness? Let me tell you: when your house is empty of basic modern conveniences (television, radio, washer, microwave, personal computer), you think that you are deprived of these luxuries. As time goes by you work hard to save money. Then, when you finally have a working refrigerator or a new sofa, you know what a blessing your life is. Wealthy people who are given everything from birth

---

[15] Editor's note: I've changed her name as well. Translated from Arabic, it means "my beloved."

are deprived of this experience—to know how hard you have worked and the difficulties you needed to overcome to secure a new life for your family. To be rich is for the soul to be rich. We were happy together, being together, being poor, and always working for a better life.

By 2000, Bashar al-Assad, the president of Syria, took the reins of power. The country's economy at first started improving, especially the median incomes for the working and middle classes. Since his economic policies seemed to be effective, and he kept radical elements in Syria in check, most people supported his policies. However, Assad also ruled with an iron fist to achieve his goals, and there were human-rights violations. He quashed freedom of speech and the right to assemble, and corruption was rampant. Still, those in power could do whatever they pleased without repercussion. Also, people were not appointed in government positions on the basis of their skill or merit. Official appointments were instead made according to the person's loyalty to the regime. To be clear, from 2000 to 2010 the problems were political rather than economic. However, by mid-2010, everything began to change; we saw a major economic downturn (and after the world started imposing sanctions on Syria because of the civil war, things got even worse). I know only what I've learned since I left Syria about the details of the so-called Arab Spring. What I knew at the time was based on much rumor and speculation. The media was controlled by the regime, so I couldn't trust what information I received from official sources. However, I will share what happened from my own experience.

2011

By March 2011, demonstrations broke out in Homs after Friday

CHAPTER THREE - HOPE

prayers. At first, demonstrators began peaceful sit-ins to call for economic reforms. Soon after, demands changed, asking for greater civil liberties, and accountability for transparency in the government. The Syrian security forces responded harshly with the demonstrations, first with tear gas, but then soon switched to live ammunition against the crowd. The Syrian security forces at the time overreacted. They panicked. Assad continued to scheme how best to suppress the demonstrators. I believe the security forces and the regime acted irrationally out of fear because they witnessed what was already happening in other countries like Libya and Tunisia, and they didn't want to lose power!

Those in charge enlisted members of sectarian groups[16] to disperse the demonstrations by terrorizing people and killing in cold blood in torture chambers those whom they considered bad apples. Also, the Syrian security forces secretly placed its members among the people to sort out who was who, to get to know the demonstrators and whoever criticized the regime by name. The day after a protest, some of my friends and acquaintances were suddenly whisked away, never to be heard from again. People started to come out regularly to join in the nightly demonstrations because of Assad's policy of violence. The people's fervor kindled a fire in the crowd's response. Things were starting to unravel because the regime answered every escalation with further escalation, tit for tat.

On April 18, 2011, a spontaneous outburst against the Syrian regime ignited a throng of protesters to take to the streets. It was late in the evening. The confidence of the people grew quickly. So many people coming together for change stirs even a coward's heart. The droves of protesters gathered in the town center, called Clock Square. They renamed it "Freedom Square."

---

[16] Note: Such as *Al Shabiha*, a group made up of mostly Alawite followers backing the Ba'athist government.

The crowd chanted in unison, "Down with Assad. Down with dictatorship! God is great!" Early in the morning of April 19th at about 2 a.m., the security forces and their thugs opened fire on the people staging the sit-in. The security forces murdered more than 300 people and severely injured countless others.[17] The residents of Homs responded with fury. Some fought back and even killed members of the security forces. The next day I went there to see for myself what had happened. The blood staining the square turned my stomach and I wondered what would become of the protests. Although I had not participated in the protests, I knew firsthand the pain. One friend from my school days was counted among those who were killed.

There was also confusion among the national army. Leaders within the ranks questioned whether they wanted to be participating in a bloodbath. Since the revolutions in the other Arab countries appeared to be successful, the regime did not want a peaceful solution. That would have meant he would have had to give in to the protesters. Instead, Assad demanded strict allegiance and threatened force against the soldiers' families if they didn't cooperate. The leaders of mosques in the city started to call for disobedience to stand up to the government's violence. The social disarray happened very quickly and people in other cities responded in shocked disbelief from afar at the violence unfurling in Homs. People spread the news through social media and word-of-mouth because the government media denied everything and claimed that the violence was part of a worldwide conspiracy against Syria. Of course, we turned on the evening news and watched, but we laughed off the ridiculous claims the announcers made. More demonstrations and more massacres soon followed. The more of these we heard about, the more the leaders, the imams, and those who stood for the

---

[17] Note: The massacre was dubbed the *Clock Massacre* because of the location of the sit-in in the Clock Square.

people called us to arms to defend our wealth, our women and children.

After both sides' leaders incited the passions of their followers, the city of Homs was lit on fire. Shelling from both sides began. We lived between a pro-government area and an area of the government opposition. Both sides fired against the other indiscriminately. We were caught in the middle.

2012

By the end of 2011, a splinter movement within the army began. Soldiers had seen the killings in cold blood (or they themselves participated in them) and had had enough. Members of the military started taking sides. Syrians began fighting other Syrians. The divisions in allegiance especially bothered the regime because it happened throughout all ranks. The events began to be covered by the media as Assad lost control of some TV and radio stations, which only further spurred people to choose a side. In my family's city quarter, a group of officers seceded from the government ranks and gathered civilians to create an armed group carrying light arms called Al Farouk Brigade. The movement was very popular among the population. They positioned themselves in the area of Baba Amr, a neighborhood southwest of the city center. This people's brigade (as well as other factions—it became confusing to keep track of them all) infuriated the regime, and in the beginning of February 2012, the war began in Baba Amr in earnest. The pro-Assad forces shelled the residents with heavy weapons. It quieted down for a few days, and then it started up again.

The cycle of fighting hard, then stopping, then starting again, seemed to be never ending. I still remember one night I spent carrying my children from the third floor of my parent's house to the ground level because of the deafening noises coming from outside. We were only two blocks away from the shells falling. The more the ground shook, the louder my children would cry. I still hear their cries today when I close my eyes at night.

At that time people only talked about the conflict. Every person had his own his opinion and political analysis. Kids made bets among each other about where the sound came from and what type of weapon made it: "That's a *Doshka*!" (A *DShK* is a Soviet-made heavy machine gun.) "There's a bomb" or "That rattling is a *500*" (an automatic weapon). It was a difficult time for kids. I've often asked myself, who will pay the price if not by death, but by the lasting hatred in the hearts of those children who managed to grow up without their parents? People held out with the notion that things would end in one month, maybe two. But the days, weeks, and months went by filled with blood, with injustice, with desperation. Despite all that, I stuck out with the belief that I would not need to leave the country. I made the choice for many reasons, but the most important was that I did not feel safe crossing a regime checkpoint. Worse yet, I could have fallen prey to forced conscription in a radical group's unit, never to see my family again. My biggest fear, though, was that my family might be stopped by one of the many foreign groups entering Syria to torture and kill us, or rape my wife.

The prison of the regime has a terrible reputation. In fact, it's a pit of despair. The stories coming out of the prisons were scary and degrading. Many people were killed under torture. Then the regime forced the families of the dead to sign a document stating that terrorist gangs had killed them. I guess the regime is covering its tracks for the possibility it survives and may face charges from an international tribunal for crimes against humanity. The choices I had were difficult. If I decided to run, I was taking a gamble; if I stayed, a shell might fall on our apartment block.

Worse still was the fear that I'd be falsely accused—many people carry a name similar to another person. Would someone mistake me for a terrorist? Would I end up in a cell and lose my fingers, one by one with a pincer? Would my wife be taken and I'd never see her again? Capricious and ridiculous accusations against innocent people were being made. I know—two neighbors disappeared in the night. If someone is wanted and his name is similar to yours, that was enough for Assad and his cronies. They'd snatch you away in the night with a bag over your head, or after you finished work when you're too tired to fight back. In Syria, the word "arrest" is even scarier than the word "war." I saw the tears of the mothers who lost their sons. If you had seen their sorrow, you would curse every international power that stood silently by when they knew about the torture chambers and the brutality of the regime.

Another important reason I didn't flee was the expense. By late 2012, to get from Homs to Italy was six thousand Euros, an amount I thought I couldn't afford. Some men made the trip and left their wives and children behind. Later they sent an application for family reunification from a European country. At the time, I couldn't bring myself to agree with that choice. For me, it seemed the coward's way out. I couldn't just leave my wife and children while I breathed the air of freedom, not even for a day. I saw the choice I thought had to make: we either live or die, but we do so together.

My indecision about fleeing however soon disappeared with a telephone call I got while I was away visiting a friend: "Raja, you have to return home … right *now!*" I was out of breath after I ran home. A crowd had gathered in my apartment and my kids were wailing. Their faces were wet, hot, and red from all the crying, and sheetrock dust covered them from head to toe. A bomb had struck next door, and shrapnel had burst into my kids' room while they were still in there. I ran upstairs to their room and I saw a broken window and glass all over the floor. The wall had a big hole in it and you could see through to the other side. Thank God, my children and neighbors were safe; no one had been hit.

I immediately changed my mind and started to think of a way to get out of Syria. My daughter and son's fear pierced a hole in my heart, and I suddenly felt selfish. How could I make them go through all this? How can I provide them with a carefree and healthy childhood without all the violence surrounding us? I knew if something happened to one of them or my wife, I would regret my insistence on staying in Homs for the rest of my life.

My new priority became the safety of my wife and children and making sure my children got a proper education. I didn't have an easy answer, though, because my savings weren't enough for even one person to travel. I struggled to find an easy answer, but there was none. The conflict inside me I now know was selfish, but at the time, I still thought staying in our home was our destiny. *I don't have the funds—God will forgive me if something happens*, I thought.

However, the situation only got worse. The shelling continued and friends still disappeared. Then, the international embargo started. My income dropped to zero, our electricity disappeared and prices for everyday groceries like fruit or milk shot through the roof. My workload also suffered—no one wants to redecorate when the walls might fall in the next day! I struggled to find a solution, a way to flee, but there wasn't one ... at least none I wanted to make.

2013

In January of 2013, a bomb exploded 300 meters from our street. The area looked like after an earthquake. Two houses were destroyed and a young girl was among the victims. A blind man died and many others were injured. I often wonder if Assad ponders all the little girls and blind men he has killed for the sake of retaining power. Were little girls and blind men such a threat to his manhood, that he commanded whole neighborhoods to be leveled?

The images we saw on social media, too, were heartbreaking and terrifying. Bombs and shells do not distinguish between children and women, an old man or an opponent. Explosives rip apart a child or a woman just as easily as they do a grown man. Everyone realized they could be partners in death. Assad applied the policy of collective punishment to all the regions where the regime lost control, despite the innocent people living in that area. The army shelled an area if citizens were reportedly carrying arms, but if there was even a hint of peaceful opposition from civilians in a particular region; the army would make arrests and torture opponents, cut off the water service and the electricity or phones. The latter policy caused suffering too, especially when they cut off the water supply.

By October of 2013, the opposition groups were successful in recruiting people from our area. Those opposition groups provided civilians with personal weapons, mostly automatic rifles and RPGs. Before then, there were few weapons in our region. Just the idea of civilians owning weapons is unthinkable for a Syrian. The consequences, unpredictable. The opposition knew it was dealing with a ruthless regime that would carpet bomb a whole city quarter because the civilians could now be counted as rebels. Still, when opposition doled out weapons, I accepted one. I suppose I thought I was protecting my family.

I managed to provide what I could for my family during this time. Some of our food came from relief organizations, but they soon stopped distributions. I suspect it was too violent for the organizations to safely deliver the provisions. Mostly people just helped each other. Many of the rich people had already fled, but some who stayed shared their wealth. By then, I had long since given up my career as a decorator. Most days, I searched for odd short-term jobs to earn money. The times were hard, but I still had my family. We didn't leave our home. I thought we would hold out. There were also glimmers of hope, too, even in the middle of the hotbed of a civil war when all we could see was the aftermath of indiscriminate violence. One such glimmer comes to mind.

In December of 2013, the army had shut off our neighborhood's water. It had happened before, but it had never lasted more than one or maybe two days. This time, almost a week had passed. Let me tell you: a person gets thirsty just from the fear that you cannot get more water. My neighbors and I put containers under the roof pipes to collect rainwater. Just when we thought all the water had run out ... snow started falling on Homs. Snow was a rare visitor to our city. My neighbors and I lost control and started laughing in joy because we knew that God had intervened. God was on our side and did not abandon us. We filled the water tanks on the rooftops with snow and we filled every available container and melted the cool blessing to drink. When you drink to spite your executioner, you consider yourself victorious. You feel something inside you grow, a strength you didn't realize you had. It's a strength that God is standing by you and you do not suffer in vain. I will never forget that snowfall and how it brought hope when everything seemed so dark.

2014

The next summer, the fighting intensified. Everyone sensed the increased tensions, and the number fleeing the violence increased as well. People sold their homes and all their belongings and simply left. One day, you saw a house filled with the business of everyday life, and people just trying to survive. The next day, the house was empty. The number of people choosing to flee increased with every passing day. By that time, many of my friends and relatives had left.

Khalila began to plead that our family should also leave. She did not grow up in a refugee camp though. I knew what difficulties a person accepts by choosing the refugee life, and I did not want that hardship for our family. I thought that if we stayed, the opportunities to rebuild our lives in Syria would be much better since a shrewd investor could maybe make a lot of money capitalizing on the low real estate prices. I figured we could tough it out. Still, I heard my children crying when the bombs fell. I was conflicted. Thinking back, my wife was right. But then, I decided we should stay. And Khalila and our children followed my lead.

2014 was a horrible year full of terrible events. Many fighting for the opposition died from the endless assaults by the regime, and both sides wreaked havoc against the innocent. Before this year, there was talk from both sides to avoid civilian areas in the conflict to try to keep them neutral and far from the fight. However, the chaos of war respects no boundaries. There is no one with whom to reason during a war. Hundreds of innocent people from my quarter died during that year. The war was definitely escalating.

2015

One evening in May of 2015, one of my younger brothers came over. He told me he had an idea. He said, "Since you do not want to leave your wife and kids in the war and have few options, how about you instead at least send your son with me?

I'm getting out of here. Your son can stay with your sister-in-law in Germany once we get to safety." (Another brother of ours had already left Syria with his family, and was safe. That brother and his family had made it to Germany, where I heard the government was giving them support.)

He continued, "After a short stay in Germany, our other brother will apply for family reunification. You'd get to travel in a safe way—you won't have to run. Besides, it won't be as expensive."

The conundrum for me was that my younger brother was fleeing illegally. He would not only be risking his own life, but also my son's. I knew what they would do: he planned on picking up my son one evening, just as the sun was setting. Then, they would have to get to Turkey to meet a smuggler. The scariest part I knew was the last step to freedom—my brother and my son would climb in a smuggler's rubber boat to cross the Mediterranean Sea to Greece. From there, the journey to Germany would be easier, but still not without peril.

My answer for my brother and his proposal at first was silence. But I considered. *Maybe it could work*, I thought.

I consulted my wife and my mother to get their opinion: "Should I take his advice and send our son?" They both agreed that it made sense to at least get one of us away from all the pain. I arrived at the conclusion that my brother's advice was the "best worst-case solution." I didn't have any other ideas, so I decided to follow through with his plan.

When the day arrived for my brother to take our son, it was very difficult to say goodbye to him. Separating from him was as if I were to lose an arm or a leg—I wouldn't feel whole without him. I feel that sometimes we're given choices we know we have to make, but making them is more than a human being can handle. I bid my ten-year-old son farewell, not knowing what the future would hold for him, or for our family.

As he was leaving I said, "I want you to grow into a man ...

I'll see you soon, buddy."

My wife, my mother and my daughter cried when he left with my brother. I tried to control myself and be strong, but I was crushed. I let go of my manhood and cried.

Five weeks later, we heard from my son. He had a harrowing journey, but also quite an adventure, meeting strangers and discovering a world with no war. We were very happy to hear that he had arrived safely. Together, my wife, my daughter, and I cried for joy. Our hope had not been in vain. At least for him.

The German government granted our son the refugee status he was seeking. He also was able to apply for us to reunite with him. At that time, we had only to wait to get an interview through aid organizations in Damascus (since the German embassy had been closed since late 2012). However, there was a problem. After the regime completely took control of the city of Homs, we began living like slaves. Personal freedom to move about, what a person could say (honestly, a few misplaced words could cost you your life), and where you could travel were up to the approval of the Syrian security. Not only that, but corruption was rampant—the only way we would have been able to access an interview to receive a pass meant handing out a load of money to grease the palms of the guards and the officials. I simply didn't have those sorts of funds.

My choice was simple (and so very hard to make too): either I sell everything I own and try to bribe the guards to get a pass to reunite with our son, or I sell everything I own and leave Syria illegally. Since there was no guarantee the officials wouldn't just take our bribe and tell us to buzz off (or worse, shoot us), I had to consider the second option, to try and run. The decision tore me apart. I could stay, having waited that long, determined to stay in my homeland, with my mother who gave me life, with the possibility that everything would work out in the end. Or I could hope the other path would be successful and flee. I would need hope if we were to flee the extreme terror and violence we had to endure each day. I prayed to God to give me an easy answer. None came. But something else did—it was a nagging feeling in my heart drawing me to trust in the hope that one day, we would be together as a family again.

I decided to opt for the second choice to hire a smuggler to flee Syria.

Khalila did not agree at first. She felt that perhaps, with the right people making the bribes, we would be able to travel. My opinion was that the risk would be too high. If we elected to try her idea, and we failed, we would be penniless and still be stuck in Homs … without our son. I finally convinced her that our best option was to flee. And hope.

September 2015

Through a clandestine, friends-and-family network, I connected with a smuggler to get us out of Syria, through Turkey, and on a boat to Greece. After I established an agreement with the smuggler, I had to shell out the money in a secure account before we could proceed. The smuggler would then receive it after we arrived safely at our destination. Our departure was difficult—we were leaving family, friends and the city we loved (even though by then it had been reduced to rubble). I told no one about our plans, except those closest to us, because to do otherwise could have made us a target for arrest. To be arrested would be the end; it meant that you could die under torture. Once you're arrested, you just disappear. Your family could assume that you probably were dead after a month or two of not hearing from you.

One lovely night late in September (it was quite warm—a good sign, I thought), we gathered up what few belongings we had left among us, bid a teary farewell to our family, and headed out on foot towards the Syrian city of Hama. My wife and daughter were traveling with me. Oddly enough, the smuggler told us we were to be escorted by a division supposedly under control by the Syrian regime. Smuggling has become a lucrative business for some divisions in the army whose loyalty to Assad had turned sour, or at least two-faced. The plan piqued my curiosity about which regime division had chosen to collaborate with the opposition groups in smuggling the people outside of the country. I only thought these questions to myself. I didn't actually ask—I didn't want to raise suspicion or cause trouble. To cause a fuss might have jeopardized our escape. I think now that some of the less loyal divisions are escorting refugees and splitting the profits with the opposition groups. But who knows. It was a confusing mess in any event. Still is.

After two days of walking and one traveling in the back of pickup trucks, our group arrived at the village of Kherbat Al Jose on the Turkish border. We were instructed by cell network and through social media to stay there in a small house and wait to attempt a border crossing through the mountains. The weather in the mountains was very cold, and there were lots of people traveling with us—at least thirty-five. We were packed in the house like canned fish.

Early one morning (it must have been 3 a.m.) the smuggler who had been communicating with us by cell phone opened the door and woke everyone up.

"Get your belongings together and be ready to go in ten minutes!" His voice startled everyone, and I jumped. I think my daughter thought we had been caught because she started crying. My wife and I calmed her, trying to reassure her that everything would be all right. The truth was, I wasn't so sure myself.

The smuggler must have known that fear is a great motivator because he had absolutely no compassion for the children and women when barking out his commands. We started out at about 3:30 a.m. and must have walked for three, maybe four hours. For me, it was a solemn scene, watching everyone head into the night, each person following the next ahead of them. We were really doing it—we were leaving our country, our homes, and lives behind.

Suddenly, we heard gunfire! It was the Turkish border patrol, just 400 meters ahead of our group. They started shooting warning shots in the air. I could see the flashes when the patrol fired their weapons, but couldn't see the soldiers themselves. The smuggler commanded us to hide between the trees and the brush until they passed. In fact, we hid for an hour and my eight-year-old daughter was grinding her teeth because of the bitter cold. I took off my coat and wrapped it around her to give her warmth. Khalila, I heard praying. At eight o'clock in the morning, we continued our journey to try and sneak by the troops, who were just on the other side of a hill (according to our smuggler, who kept running ahead to scout a clear path.)

We went around a ravine, and the morning sun was already high above the mountains in the distance. When we got around to the other side, our group was ambushed by the Turkish border patrol. They commanded us to put our hands up and marched us two kilometers to the border. Each member of our little group was exhausted because the terrain was mountain-ous and rugged. We returned to the little house where we had started our first attempt at a border crossing and waited for another opportunity.

The next day, we made another attempt. However, this time we tried another route; the smuggler guided us through a valley. Again, he woke us early in the morning, but a bit earlier, around 1 a.m. This time our journey was more difficult than the first attempt because we had to trudge through roads filled with mud. Lots of people complained under their breath, but I didn't say anything. I'm proud of my wife and daughter for holding their tongues too. This was no pleasure cruise—we were running for our lives! After walking for approximately six hours, our shoes caked with sticky mud like day-old hummus to dry bread, we successfully crossed the border. Then the smuggler told us to sit down, all of us, right where we were. He extorted us, forcing every person to pay $100, even women and children; otherwise, he'd make us head back to Syria. We complied. What choice did we have? It was either obey him and get to a bus that would take us to the border town Antakya, or head back to Syria and try again on our own. We had few options and he wanted our money.

When we arrived in Antakya, he extorted us again for $100 in order to take us to Izmir, a city that shares the water border with Greece. Again, we paid. Honestly, by this time I was worried that I wouldn't have enough money to make it. I hoped and prayed that God would soften the smuggler's heart to allow us to keep traveling if things got worse and I couldn't pay. But I just didn't know what would happen.

After we arrived at Izmir, the smuggler reminded us of our plan: he would help us cross the sea in inflatable boats. Of course, he did not tell us where we'd be headed, only that we were going to Greece. Many of us still had our cell phones with us and the smuggler didn't want any of us leaking the information to anyone. He didn't want to get caught. When we got to the seashore, we saw another guy sitting in an idling truck in the distance. Besides the guy driving the truck, the beach was completely abandoned. Again, we traveled by night. There may have been people around, but they were all sleeping, I assume.

Then I finally saw the "Dracula" that every refugee fears—the inflatable rubber boat that I saw the guy unloading from the back of the truck. These boats can hardly be called boats at all; they're not intended to carry as many people the smuggler tries to stuff on them. For him, it's all about profit. To maximize his profits, he wants to maximize the group size. Safety isn't his ultimate concern. Like any businessman, he can deal with some losses if they are manageable. This Dracula was a little over six meters in length. As our company of terrified refugees continued to approach the truck, I looked at the size of the group: thirty-five. *How are we all going to fit on that thing?* Then I looked out to the sea. The Mediterranean Sea is no calm lake. It's really a *sea*. I had heard the stories of some refugees who had died sitting on that terrible little Dracula, having to watch their sons and daughters fall into the water and no one was there to rescue them. Yes, there is a reason why this yellow rubber boat is called "Dracula"—he will suck all hope of rescue from you if you give him the chance.

Then the smuggler told us to prepare ourselves and put on life jackets, (which we had to purchase—nothing was free), and head to the boat next to the truck to help unload it. We had only just pushed off from shore before a powerboat suddenly appeared from around a point with its lights on and Turkish officers howling commands from a loudspeaker. Again, we were stopped. The Turkish Coast Guard in the powerboat approached our inflatable craft, and a car drove on the rocky shore from the beach where we cast off. They confiscated our life jackets and asked us to pledge that we will not try again. Surprisingly, they didn't arrest us, but just let us go. We returned to Izmir to wait for another attempt to cross the sea to Greece.

While we waited, I checked the weather conditions on the Internet and social media. Two days after our first attempt, the smuggler said he'd be trying again, but it was rainy and the forecast indicated that the waves' height would reach 80 cm, which wasn't safe for a flimsy inflatable boat. To add insult to injury, it was pouring rain and very cold. I looked at my wife; her face was stern and she shook her head. According to the information I'd read online, you can sail safely only when the height of the waves do not exceed 20 cm. I refused to leave. The smuggler can't force you to leave because the money is with a third party and he won't get it until you reach Greece safely.

The smuggler told us we would have to wait three days for the next group to arrive. I got to thinking how much we paid him and did a quick calculation in my head: if this man got just half of the refugees safely to their destination in a month, he had to be clearing over $40,000 per month after bribes and expenses. For a Syrian during wartime, that is a lot of money! After hearing my insistence that my family wouldn't board the boat, the smuggler shrugged and told us to return to the hiding place in Izmir to wait for instructions.

It turned out to be a good thing we didn't board the boat that time because the Turkish Coast Guard stopped them again. This time they arrested those who left on that night. I suppose they hauled the people back to the Syrian border. Had we gone with that group, I'm sure we wouldn't have made it. But after four days hiding like rats in Izmir, we finally made a last-ditch attempt. It was now or nothing. My daughter and wife were growing weary of waiting. Plus, we all smelled quite bad—none of us had had a bath or shower since we left Homs.

After arriving at a new point of departure (smugglers must shift the launching sites to avoid detection), we saw again our "Dracula." This time, it was one meter shorter than the last boat we had tried to board four days earlier. This time, we had more people clamoring to board it too.

When we got to the boat, the smuggler commanded us all to board. People argued with him that the boat was too small. We couldn't all fit! He said that children and smaller people should sit on their parents' laps. (These guys seriously have no concern for you. They only want your money.)

We were lucky. A family of six refused to board the boat with so many people. My wife patted the shoulder of my daughter and encouraged her saying, "Get on now. We are going to freedom." We shoved off.

The trip was full of tension and the sea was scary at night. Women and children were praying to God. Several times we saw lights in the distance, but none of the boats approached us. I kept wondering if all my hopes would be dashed in this moment. I feared the Dracula would burst, and the water was only 25 centimeters from the lip of the boat's edge. Several times, the sea rushed into the boat from waves and people started yelling. If too much water got in, it would only accelerate our demise since the weight of the boat would become even greater. In times like these, people try to work together. I believe they are doing so out of self-preservation, but they know that their fate is yours as well. You're all in the same boat!

After two hours of this tense ordeal, we arrived on the Grecian shores. We were in Europe. We were free. Arriving there alive was an indescribable moment of joy for everyone. Women, children, and men alike were crying. People were praising God, that God had spared them to survive not only the escape from the pain of Syria, but also to find a new life of freedom, hoping one day to return. The people forgot all the agony we had gone through. I will never forget the sound of our boat—the Dracula that had decided to let us go—as its bottom slid onto the sandy beach on that Greek island.

A European team came to our rescue. They said, "Welcome to Greece. We love you all. We want to help you." The members of the rescue team had blankets, food, and water. They gave it all to us. I embraced one of the men, thanking him for everything. He said, "No problem!" (in English) and he smiled. They told us we had landed on the island of Samos. Since our harrowing journey and ecstatic rescue, I've come to learn that the smuggler had been giving reports and that a rescue team had been following our progress on Facebook. The rescue teams have made it their mission to reach out and help everyone who is running from the violence in their homeland. They continue to do so, even though the tiny island of Samos and many other Greek islands have become overwhelmed from all the people fleeing Syria. I was reminded that God has placed good people everywhere.[18]

After presenting our papers, they gave us a document for each person with his or her photo and personal information. Then, after we received this refugee-status card, we traveled by bus to the Greek capital, Athens, and then to a refugee camp in the port of Athens. We were alive but living once again in a refugee camp. It seemed my life had come full circle.

Today

My wife, Khalila, my daughter, and I still live in Greece, in the refugee camp in the port of Athens. Our son still is with my sister-in-law and brother, stuck in Germany. The living conditions are difficult. We lack many resources that we had taken for granted, even in the Syrian war zone. I am speaking of the illusion of "European human rights." Sometimes, I can't believe we're living in the 21st century. How is it possible that a country such as Greece, that claims to honor human rights, fails to provide the simplest necessities, like hot water for a shower? Despite the fact that we did not come to Europe for its legendary dining, in the camp the food is extremely bad. Often the milk, eggs, or bread they give us have gone bad. Disease is rampant. And no matter how much complaining, pleading, or polite requesting I do, nothing seems to help. We are stuck here. I began to wonder a year ago whether we would ever see our son again. We also have nothing to do in the camp. An idle mind can only think of its suffering.

The misery only gets worse each day. At first, it's a nuisance. Then it becomes a real bother. Soon, you're ready to strangle

---

[18] Note: YouTube® provides many videos of refugees first contact with Greece. Many are exceptionally heart-wrenching and worth watching.

someone. People who sleep at night bother you in the day. People who sleep during the day bother you at night. You have to put up with foul language coming from the adjoining tent—you speak loudly so your children do not hear it. You have to deal with the cultural differences between people, or put up with hordes of people waiting in line to use the bathroom (thirty minutes, minimum). You have to put up with your kids' demands and deal with your own seesawing emotions. Truthfully, the difficulty I'm referring to is due only to the mismanagement of the camp, and not the Greek people, who have been very welcoming. Strangers help you all the time when you meet them on the street or on buses. The Greek people smile and accept you.

We met a young Greek man who works as a rescuer and volunteer. His mission is to serve humanity. He helped us get an appointment at the German embassy in Athens, and showed us the landmarks and historical sites. He continues to be in regular contact with us. I feel the problem lies not with individuals, but with faceless institutions and impenetrable government policies.

We fled our homeland, asking for protection from the hell of war. Syrians are an educated people and we have a strong work ethic. Many of us in the camp worked very hard to achieve success in our fields of work. Doctors, teachers, nurses, architects, and tradesmen now all live together in this camp, in squalor. It seems like we have been forgotten. I don't think it is too much to ask for hot water and unspoiled provisions. There are foul characters among the refugees, too, but they do not represent the majority.

I want you to know my story, and to know our suffering. Many of us are stuck at the border and people need to know that we're still here. We need your help. My will to go on wears thinner with each passing day. All that remains is my hope that you will be moved by my story and advocate for change.

I am a human being just like you; God chose my birthplace to be the Syrian city of Homs. It is a city close to God and many people who call it home are kind, compassionate souls. I was born into a poor family. I had to face the difficulties of life and poverty. I had to run from my home. Know that no refugee does so because he believes that he wants to take advantage of your economy or steal your jobs. The only reason we ran to risk death on a rubber boat is because a much more terrible monster called war chased us away from our homeland.

One day, I hope to return to our home with every member in my family accounted for. I've spent every penny I have to run, and now we're broke. We see few options for our family reunification because for us to get to our son, we need money I do not have. To make matters worse, things are deteriorating in Europe. Hatred and terrorism seem to be everywhere, and Europe looks as though it's falling apart at the seams. In times like these, I feel lost. I consider that God perhaps did not save us so much from the death in Syria, but needs us to endure more trials, more suffering, here in Greece. For what, though? I don't see any answers.

The one hopeful trace I see each morning is when I wake to see my daughter's face. Sometimes, she crawls over her bed to climb into ours to slide in between her mother and me. I hear her breathing slowly. Most of the time she falls back asleep.

Several months ago, she didn't fall asleep. She was restless and chatty.

"Papa, when will we leave the camp to go back home?" she asked.

"I don't know. It depends on what the government decides what will happen to us," I said.

She lay still for a minute, then said, "Why does the government decide what will happen to us—to send us where we belong—when they know that we live in Homs?"

I said, "Because the government knows there is still war. You don't want to go back to war, do you?"

She again lay still.

My wife turned and joined the conversation: "When so many powers are concerned for our fate, it is difficult for them all to decide what to do with us."

My daughter said, "I know there is only one power, God. He knows we belong together, at home."

I have not forgotten our conversation. It is the simple vision only a child can offer: the hope that one power—God, who has no regulations or political squabbles—can unite a family so far from home. Her hope remains my hope today as well—that everything will work out, eventually.

Raja was desperate to get his message to me. It was clear he is extremely frustrated with his family's current living situation in the Greek refugee camp. Yet despite his aggravation, he insisted that he hasn't lost hope. His spiritual asset, hope, serves as the foundation undergirding his continued resilience to endure in the face of stress—from the simple inconveniences of living in a refugee camp to the trauma of leaving behind his homeland, and the fact that his son still lives a thousand miles away from him and his wife.

I asked Raja about the how the war progressed from his perspective. Other than few headlines and articles I had read about the Syrian civil war, I didn't realize how exceptionally complicated the conflict was and continues to be. Raja himself admitted that it was difficult to keep up with any specific group's professed loyalties because the civil war is a continually mutating state of affairs. Ever since *Daesh* (what most Americans know as ISIS or ISIL—the group began fighting in earnest in about April of 2013) inserted themselves in the Syrian conflict, the war has taken on a puzzle-like quality that is as complicated in its comprehension as it is convoluted in its potential international repercussions. From what I gathered from Raja, it's a huge mess with no foreseeable end. The war's unpredictable outcome made me even more curious about Raja's hope and how it sustains his resilience. I asked him how his hope impacts his will to keep going, to persevere, in the face of his daily hardships.

He said, "I've lost everything and our son lives in Germany while we're stuck in a refugee camp in Greece. Still, I am happy. Do you know why? Because I believe we one day will be together as a family again, living in Syria."

I asked Raja how he could believe that his living situation would improve when his experience up to today has been so unpredictable. He responded, "God tests us often in this life. We have to steer our responses thoughtfully ... with wisdom, patience, love, and above all, hope. We all have to pay a price for God to carry out God's justice in the world."

"Is that how you see everything you've had to go through—as a test from God?" I asked.

He said, "Yes. It is a test. It is also not something God has given us directly. No. I do not believe that God makes people act so selfishly."

I asked him to say more.

"I believe ... God does not select people to be puppets. For example, the smuggler who extorted us several times as we fled Syria: he did not receive his commands from God! No. He did so out of his own greed. I suppose you could say that God was aware of the larger picture of our desperate circumstances and that was our test—to see if we'd learn to hope and trust God."

As I read Raja's responses to my questions, I was learning how hope served as his spiritual asset, how it bolstered his resilience, so he could keep fighting to wake up each day and face it boldly, no matter what difficulties he might have to overcome. Raja was insistent that hope isn't a magic wand to make everything better. Instead, his hope provides him a meaning or purpose: to fight for justice. For him, that meant sharing his story with me.

He said, "When we arrived in the refugee camp in Greece, everything was bad. We did not expect such poor conditions. We had to put up with crowds and bad smells. The food was also poor quality. Even the international oversight groups agreed—some food isn't even fit for a dog! We had to take cold showers and we live shoulder to shoulder with strangers in a tent. Some of them have diseases too, like tuberculosis or hepatitis-C. I don't like living here. No one does! A tiny bit of my hope has already been realized, though, because you will publish my story."

Mentioning to him that although I hoped millions would read his story, I knew the stark reality is that the readership probably would number only a couple thousand. "It doesn't matter if only ten people read about my life. So be it. Then, God *wills* that ten more people will know our suffering," he said.

"Why is important that people know your suffering or your story?" I asked.

"Because then maybe things will change, of course! My hope is our situation will change."

I never questioned Raja's sincerity in hoping his situation might change. However, I wanted to know more how his hope undergirds his will to go on. Does he persevere *because* of hope? Or does he wake each day and face it simply because there isn't any other reason to live than to just face life on its own terms?

I asked him, "I've defined *spiritual assets* as virtues or gifts that allow a person to see more clearly, love more deeply and act more courageously. How does hope accomplish these things for you?" His answer was compelling because it sounded similar to a passage out of the Christian scriptures, 1 John 4:19, "We love, because [God] first loved us."

"One morning in the refugee camp, about a month ago, I

woke up after seeing my father in my dream. He looked just the way he did before he died. I still love my father, but he is gone. Does our love disappear after our loved ones die? No! Our love for them goes on. The same is with these spiritual assets you talk about. Does my hope disappear, just because I'm terrified that the [rubber boat] will sink in the sea? No. My hope goes on."

"The dream I had of my father reminded me of his strength, patience, and love for God. Oh God, what is this strength that you gave your worshippers? Even after death, love transforms our weakness to strength. Those times when my father was still alive were filled with joyful poverty. At that time, I thought everyone was capable of feeling joy. It did not matter how little a person had. I didn't expect that one day I would have to answer questions about that period in the context of happiness. Tests from God for us in this life are many. We all have to steer ourselves with wisdom, patience, and love. We all have to pay the price for God to enact justice in this world. May my beloved father rest in peace, and may God grant him residence in paradise.

"My friend, I'm telling you my hope for a better life is the continuation of my father's hope for me. I love my family because my father first loved his own. He loved me. The hope for a better world may not come for me, personally, but I do hope that if it does not follow for me, it will come for my children and grandchildren. That keeps me going."

Interviewing Raja taught me that his hope stems directly from his faith in God as a dedicated Muslim. "How does your Muslim upbringing affect your hope to continue on, despite the poor conditions you're living in?" I asked.

"Daniel, my friend, our relationship with God is the base for everything, even for hope. Islam, at its heart, is a religion about our submission to God, whose heart pumps with the blood of hope and love. Islam is not connected in any way with terrorism, whether military or intellectually. These terrorists only claim to be acting for God, but they are not. They are apostates. God is the only one that brings happiness after sadness, but only evil people bring sadness and terror after happiness.

"I am waiting to see my son soon. This was my first objective since [my family] left Syria. In the meantime, I believe God gave me a different mission, one I hadn't thought of: that I would need to live through a bit of suffering so that you'd share my story. Hopefully, people will read it and know the suffering the Syrian people have gone through. So, my hope rests that people's hearts will be moved to [change the world] to become a better place."

Hope and Resilience

Hope is difficult to differentiate from resilience because *resilience*—the ability to bounce back after stress or trauma—depends on the conviction that survival is even possible. The opposite of hope is despair or meaninglessness. Human beings cannot live sustainably without hope because, in its absence, we cannot fathom what the abyss of a life without meaning or purpose looks like. This lack of hope (or meaning or purpose) is what Viktor Frankl, the Swiss psychologist who endured the Nazi holocaust, called the "existential vacuum."

Frankl wrote as much about the lack of hope in his great work *Man's Search for Meaning*. He recalled how the despair of a friend who had lost hope ultimately doomed him:

> Those who know how close the connection is between the state of mind of a man—his courage and hope, or lack of them—and the state of immunity of his body, will understand that the sudden loss of hope and courage can have a deadly

effect. The ultimate cause of my friend's death was that the expected liberation did not come and he was severely disappointed. This suddenly lowered his body's resistance against the latent typhus infection. His faith in the future and his will to live had become paralyzed and his body fell victim to illness.[19]

Our resilience depends on hope, the belief that the storm is temporary and worth enduring for the reward of a new day after its passing. Frankl indicated the positive aspects of hope bring meaningfulness and purposefulness for a person to push forward, despite the hardships they must endure:

> We must never forget that we may also find meaning in life even when confronted with a hopeless situation, when facing a fate that cannot be changed. For what then matters is to bear witness to the uniquely human potential at its best, which is to transform a personal tragedy into a triumph, to turn one's predicament into a human achievement. When we are no longer able to change a situation— just think of an incurable disease such as inoperable cancer —we are challenged to change ourselves.[20]

With every roadblock Raja came up against, he had to hold out in the hope God has the power to bring about good, even through horrific circumstances, and that God can and *does* work through those circumstances to bring about God's will,

---

[19] Frankl, Viktor. E. 1992. *Man's Search for Meaning.* Boston: Beacon Press. 84.
[20] Ibid. 116.

mysterious as it may be. Raja's strength (and his resilience to live) seem to come from his belief that God wants him to endure through the struggles so that you will come to know his story and the tribulations of the Syrian people, and that he will one day be reunited with his family and allowed to return to his homeland.

From my experience standing in a cell in a North Dakota jailhouse, wearing an anti-suicide smock, I can relate to Raja's hope. I asked myself what I think anyone would ask in that situation—*what now?* I prayed in that moment, and just as Raja received no easy answers handed down from above, I didn't get any either. Yet, I still had hope. I hoped that I'd be able to manage to stay sober for just one day, and that one day, God could use me for good again. That hope gave me a reason to live and a purpose to commit to. My hope was the only thing I had to hang onto.

Many definitions of hope use the metaphors of darkness and light, an apt description when you consider that in darkness, you cannot see, but in the light you can. For Raja, life was dark when he feared a shelling would cause his roof to fall in and kill his children. The darkness continues when your food is spoiled, you have to wait a half-hour in line to pee, and the only option for bathing is a cold shower. Desmond Tutu said, however, "Hope is being able to see that there is light despite all of the darkness."[21] The Dalai Lama also offers this wisdom: "The very purpose of our life is happiness, which is sustained by hope. We have no guarantee about the future, but we exist in the hope of something better."[22]

---

[21] Solomon, Deborah. 2007. ""The Priest"." *The New York Times Magazine*, March 7. MM12.

[22] Unknown. 2013. *His Holiness The 14th Dalai Lama of Tibet.* May 19. Accessed September 20, 2016. http://www.dalailama.com/news/post/950-the-tulane-unified-commencement-ceremony-and-a-public-talk-at-the-lakefront-arena.

These wise teachers focus on the light beyond that can be reached *through the darkness itself.* I'm convinced Raja believes as much as well. With hope, we see a future filled with light once again, not out of wishful thinking, but in trust that the struggle will be worthwhile, meaningful. Hope lives in the sure and certain belief that, one day, light will shine. Hope is more than an aid to assist you through the darkness; hope gives you the strength to overcome life's darkness. The Islamic scholar, writer, and teacher Yasmin Mogahed described hope as pearls lying on the dark ocean floor.

> The amazing thing about the floor of the ocean [is that] no light enters it. But, that dark place isn't the end. Remember that the darkness of night precedes the dawn. And as long as your heart still beats, this is not the death of it. You don't have to die here. Sometimes, the ocean floor is only a stop in the journey. And it is when you are at this lowest point, that you are faced with a choice. You can stay there at the bottom until you drown, or you can gather pearls and rise back up—stronger from the swim, and richer from the jewels.[23]

With hope, we can envision a future beyond the darkness and endure the gloom as we await another, brighter day. Raja's hope isn't just trite optimism. Raja's hope that he will eventually reunite his family gives him meaning and purpose—the resilience to keep on going through the darkness. His hope comes from his understanding that God is ultimately in control and that, even through his fears and daily frustrations, he

---

[23] Mogahed, Yasmin. 2011. *The Ocean of Dunya, Part II.* November 13. Accessed September 20, 2016. http://www.yasminmogahed.com/2011/11/13/take-back-your-heart/

can trust God to make things right again. That trust in God is what drives his hope. Light, even the smallest glow or flicker, always overcomes darkness.

Figures 1 - 32

Introduction

Figures 1-3: The irony is that most of my life has been "normal." However, even when these photos had been taken, my addiction was already brewing.

Figure 4: The author with his boys
at the publication of his first book
Sobriety: A Graphic Novel.

Chapter One

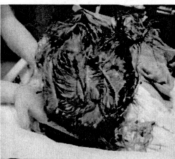

Figures 5-7: Cathy's injuries from her attack were both gruesome and life changing. Her attackers' damage with a machete scarred her for life.

Figure 8: Cathy one day prior to her attack.

Figure 9: Recent photograph. She has survived and thrives.

Chapter Two

Figure 10: Map of Iraq showing cities Hunter operated in. *(Source: AP)*

Figures 11 & 12: A soldier's life depends on being able to blend into his or her surroundings. Companies must operate as a single, cohesive unit. *(Source: AP)*

Chapter Three

Migrant arrivals in Greece by sea

Arrivals in 2015
856,723

Total arrivals by
sea in 2016
123,246

Number of people
· 1,000
● 10,000
50,000
100,000

BULGARIA
MACEDONIA
Idomeni border crossing
Kavala
Istanbul
ALBANIA Thessaloniki
GREECE
TURKEY
Izmir
Athens
Bodrum

Source: UNHCR (data to 1 March 2016)

Figure 13: Map of flight routes from Syria.
(Source: UNHCR)

Figure 14: Children living
amongst the rubble of war in
Syria. *(Source: AP)*

Figure 15: Pre- and postwar
photos of Homs. *(Source: AP)*

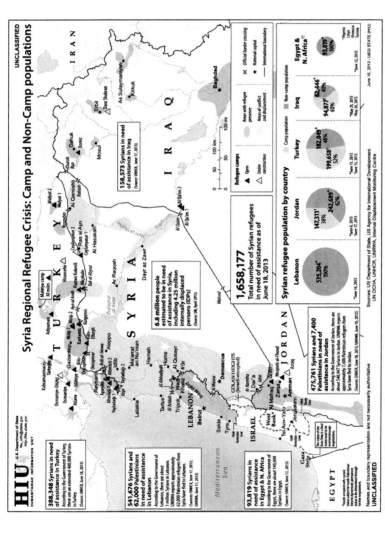

Figure 16: Syrian refugee crisis in the Middle East. *(Sources listed.)*

Chapter Four

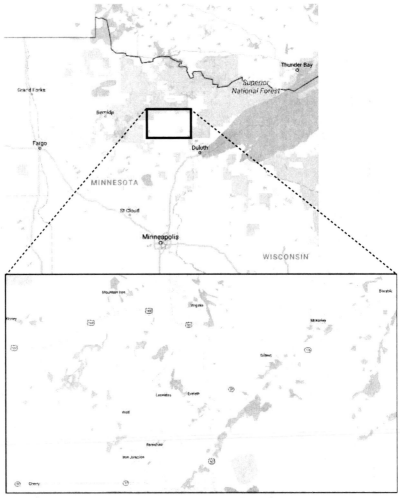

Figure 17: Map of Minnesota and inset of Iron Range towns where Kitty lived. *(Source: Google Maps.)*

Figure 18: Graduation photo of Linda, Kitty's sister.

Figure 19: Craig walking Kitty's daughter Heather down the aisle.

Figure 20: Craig and Kitty shortly before Craig's death.

Figure 21: The Author and Kitty at her northern Minnesota home.

Chapter Five

Figure 22: The Reverend Richard W. Rouse, author of *Fire of Grace: The Healing Power of Forgiveness.*

Chapter Six

Figures 23 & 24: Michael as a toddler and a mother's love for her son.

Figure 25: Michael and Jennifer.

Figure 26: A more recent photo of Michael.

Chapter Four

Faith

Interviewing a person is like dancing with a new partner: you need to notice the cues the other is giving in order to move naturally together. A dance, as well as an interview, can come off as forced, making a pair stumble while dancing, and leaving an interview feeling artificial. However, sometimes a natural rapport between people makes an interview flow like an old couple whirling gracefully on a ballroom floor. My conversation with Kitty Fallgren felt like an elegant waltz because she naturally radiates kindness, patience, and grace. She was easy to talk with and listen to.

I had traveled from Saint Paul, Minnesota, to a little town just outside of Brainerd in the northern part of the state, the locale the Coen brothers used as the setting for their film *Fargo*. Like the movie scenes, the area is densely wooded with pine trees that camouflage the size of the population in that area as you drive through it—nearly 65,000 people live in Crow Wing County. Kitty's home is tucked away at the end of a cul-de-sac overgrown with pine trees and an undergrowth of buckthorn. When I entered, she greeted me and offered me a cup of warm tea. As we retired to a small, sunlit side room, she brought out a stack of papers, documents she had collected, police statements, and copies of letters she had written and began to tell me her story.

Kitty's story is heart-rending but no less hopeful and heartening. She grew up in a tumultuous household. Her family moved every couple of years, apparently to relocate to a place where her mother or father hadn't yet destroyed any relationships.

As she recounted her story, it surprised me that as a kid she thought her family situation was normal. I suppose it shouldn't have caught me off guard. After all, what should a child believe is normal if all she's ever known is chaos and abuse? The other aspect of her story a person might not expect to hear is that she has grown into a woman of deep faith with an unwavering conviction of God's grace. It's especially surprising since Kitty hadn't grown up with a faith community to guide her, nor did her parents or siblings provide a cornerstone upon which to construct any belief system. Where did her understanding of a gracious God come from? More importantly, how—if at all—did Kitty's faith positively affect her resilience, her ability to keep on going, even in the worst of circumstances?

What I discovered is that faith doesn't arise out of a vacuum. The writer of the New Testament letter to the Hebrews speaks of a "cloud of witnesses"—people from the Old Testament who held onto a courageous faith, even when they didn't know the outcome. Through Kitty's story, I also learned that many simple, small acts of kindness a person experiences along their life's path provide encouragement to persevere. Kitty's faith makes her resilience not only robust, but also inspiring when you know her story and what she's been through.

Kitty's Story

I grew up in a family where secrets were a way of life. *Don't tell* was something we lived with every day. Of course, this was an unspoken rule, but we learned to follow it. Telling my story today still feels like I'm betraying my family by saying anything. Each of my family remembers the story differently, and today when I talk about it with my siblings, conflicts arise. I've tried to write notes about my past before, and I can't tell you how many times I've had to stop after I've started talking about it because the emotions it brought up were just too hard to deal with.

I was born on the Minnesota Iron Range in a little town, Eveleth, just a bit over a half-an-hour's drive from Bob Dylan's hometown, Hibbing. My mom's name was Vivian and my dad's Donald. We moved around a lot, always to towns out there in the sticks on the Iron Range. I have trouble remembering where I was when, because we moved so often.

My dad was an alcoholic. I think you can guess one of the reasons we moved a lot was that my dad burned a lot of bridges. But he was a hard worker; he always worked. Never got fired from a job. When my mom told my grandma that she was thinking about getting a divorce, my grandma said to her, "Now why would you want to do that? He's a good provider. You should stick with him." Still, my dad managed to ruffle plenty of feathers after he was done working and hit the bottle hard. Later, after my mom divorced him, she had her own issues with attaching herself to abusive men then leaving to find the next one to glom onto. So we moved, time and again. I was eight years old when my mom left my dad.

I had seven brothers and sisters. My mom's first she gave up for adoption. We call him Patrick, even though that's not really his name. Then there's my sister Dawn. She is the oldest girl. After her, came my sister Linda, who died when she was eighteen; she was murdered down in Minneapolis. My sister Wendy just passed away a year ago. She was a musician and an amazing person. After her came my brother Steve, who's a free spirit and kind of just floats around and does what he does. Then my brother Danny died right after he was born. Three years after Danny, I was born. I have one younger sister, Peggy.

Soon after Linda had been killed, my mom and dad got a divorce. Even though my parents were separated, I still often saw my dad, and not because of the court-ordered visitation. No. It was more informal. I suppose it didn't help that my grandma—my mom's mother—still welcomed my dad in her house, even after the divorce. I think that really hurt my mom that my dad was still considered a part of the family. My dad came to visit us at our house too. And, as is always the case with a disease like alcoholism, my dad's drinking affected our whole family. Before my parents split, some things happened that shouldn't have happened. Alcoholism blurs boundaries, and my dad crossed them more than once. I have little recall about the details, but I know it happened.

Before Linda was killed, when our dad was still married to our mom, I know he was "bothering" Linda and my sister Dawn. Dad would come into my sister Wendy's room too. To this day, she denies that anything ever happened. But I remember one night where she showed me a knife she kept under her pillow. I asked her why she had a knife, and she told me, "To keep him away." Later, when I spoke with my nieces, they confirmed that their mother had told them about my dad's behavior. They also said that when Dad would show up at their place, my sister Wendy would have her kids hide from him.

As I mentioned, something happened between my dad and me too when I was very young, but I can't remember exactly what. Later, when I was in my twenties, a friend from school and I went out to see the house where we used to live. When we got to the house and were walking down the road, the closer we got, the worse I started to feel inside. It was a sense of dread. There was another building beside the house, and my friend said, "Well, you know, let's go over there. Isn't that a sauna?" And I couldn't do it. It was like my feet were just frozen to the ground. Then I remembered that we used to have chickens next to the sauna and I used to feed them. I could not even go peek in the window of the sauna. I felt sick.

Later in life, my mom wrote me a letter. She said that she didn't know all the funny business my dad was doing. And she wrote that she didn't know about what happened in the sauna until much later on. She was the one who mentioned the sauna in her letter, not me. But I believe our family lived in its secrets. My mom, I think, kept the secrets to protect us, but her hiding didn't do that at all. Instead, those secrets went down deep inside of my siblings and me, and they ate at us. I know they did for me, at least. That's the thing about secrets—they never seem to go away.

Even recently, I think my mom wanted to protect my dad and denied all that was going on because it wasn't just Wendy who kept a knife under her pillow. My older sisters did that too. (I think that's where Wendy got the idea.) In Linda's senior year, before she moved away and was murdered, my mom had been working in Aurora at a restaurant; I suppose she wanted to get out of the house and try to earn some extra money. My dad came home and he began to bother Linda in her bedroom, but she reached under her pillow and stabbed him in the arm with a butcher knife. My dad had to go to the emergency room and get stitches. My mom had "forgotten" about this incident and only remembered it much later after I told her about it. She said, "Oh yes … now I remember that. I suppose your dad … well, he did some things."

Before my sister Linda was murdered, she wrote a poem about our family when she was in high school:

Family Games

The members of our family play
An evil little game.
Its purpose is destruction,

Torture is its name.

Each person has a special place
A position that he plays.
He tries to cause all the hurt he can
In this cruel and hopeless maze.

Our world is full of sorrow
And large amounts of sin.
Around the corner lurks a creature, "Spite."
It's a game you just can't win.

There may be a lack of happiness,
But there is no lack of fear.
I'm afraid of what they're doing to me.
I must get away from here.

Shortly after Linda wrote this poem, she graduated from high school and moved to Minneapolis. I know now she wanted to get away from Dad. At the time, I thought that's just what people do—they move on, and they keep the secrets hidden deep down inside. I was only eight when Linda moved away.

Less than six months after Linda graduated from high school, a mentally disturbed man entered her apartment in Minneapolis and strangled her to death. She had just turned eighteen. Because I was so young at the time—and also because our family didn't talk about such things—I didn't know any of the details about what had happened. Later on, I became obsessed with finding out. Back then, though, it was all so unreal. I kept thinking that she would walk in the door one day to give me a hug. I never got a hug from Linda, of course, but neither did I get one from anyone else. Not until much later in my life.

Recently, I've been able to piece together what happened from a confession of the murderer that I obtained from the police interview, statements from her neighbors, and her autopsy report. Here's what I now know: a serial killer murdered Linda. His name was David Torgerson. He was a disturbed man from the beginning. He had almost killed a young girl when he was a teenager; she survived. He floated in and out of institutions in his late teens and early twenties. Soon after he was released from the state hospital in Rochester, Minnesota, in the summer of 1968, he strangled a waitress just getting off work in a parking ramp. He thought he had killed her, but she survived too.

I learned his first successful murder was my sister in 1969. She was in her apartment on Chicago Avenue in Minneapolis. She lived on the top floor of her building. Torgerson had gotten one of his "urges" to kill a woman, any woman, and had randomly selected Linda's apartment. At about 10:30 at night, he knocked on the door. Linda answered it and asked what he wanted. He forced himself into her apartment and began strangling her on the kitchen floor. He then filled up a bathtub to finish the job (I guess he wasn't sure if she was dead and he wanted to drown her), but Linda was already dead from the strangling. I discovered that it was my aunt, who lived near the Twin Cities, who went to Minneapolis to identify Linda's body at the morgue. I don't know why my mother or father didn't make the trip, but I can guess—it was just too difficult for either of them to carry out.

Torgerson would go on to strangle another woman, Julie Mehrman, 19, that summer in Minneapolis; then another, Becky Hansen, 19, in Rochester in 1970. Authorities believe he may be tied to two additional murders in Minnesota prior to 1973. He also had murdered his wife, Lana, her two children, Sylvia and John, and a babysitter, Rebecca Rathbun. He was finally caught in July of 1973 when he attempted to assault a young woman in a VW bus in Michigan and was stopped by a man named Bob Boelens. Boelens held Torgerson until the police arrived. Shortly after, Torgerson made his confession to the police about the previous murders he'd committed. I suppose he confessed because he was proud that he had gotten away with them. Then, before he got to trial, he hung himself in his jail cell. All told, Torgerson had murdered at least seven people, possibly up to nine.

I guess I'm thankful that he confessed to the police. Without his confession, I wouldn't know the details I do today about my sister's death. It's helped me gain some closure for my loss. Back when she was killed, I didn't know anything other than I would never see my sister again.

The tragedy of Linda's death threw my family into a tailspin, and with it, my childhood as well. We didn't have a faith in God to comfort us, and our parents soon divorced. My older sisters Dawn and Wendy both got married and soon after had babies. Neither of their marriages lasted. After my parents' divorce, we moved to Biwabik into a trailer in my grandma's back yard. Later, we shifted from one community to another every year or two. We wandered around so often because my mom didn't get just boyfriends; she got husbands. The rest of us had to move on to the next "father" too. We lived mostly in trailers, some apartments, and a few houses here and there.

I think as far as my mom was concerned, my sister's murder was done and over. It was in the past; it didn't need to be talked about. My mother never offered me a real explanation of what happened. All she said was, "That guy who murdered Linda is so mentally ill, there's no need for him to be punished because he's had enough punishment in his life already." In fact, recently, when I finally had gone through all the material with the police to discover the real story, one officer sent me an email telling me that he was sorry for my loss. That email—nearly 50 years later—was the first time anybody had actually told me they understood and felt sorry for my pain. His words made such an impact on my life. Don't misunderstand; I loved my mother very much, despite her failings. However, she saw the world in very black-and-white terms; there were no gray areas in her understanding how the world should work. Now I think my mother was trying hard, and the only way she knew how to live was in the black-and-white. She worked really hard at being a mom. Her central identity was grounded in being a mother and providing for us any way she could. I believe that's why she attached herself so quickly to men who took advantage of her, and us kids too.

My early school years were filled with distrust. I had a difficult enough time making friends on account of the constant moving around we did, but also since I was naturally shy and insecure. I knew evil existed in this world, and I knew in my heart that I must be a bad person too, because of what my dad did to me. I didn't expect that anyone would want to know the "real" me. My surrogate fathers (and my real father who kept drifting in and out of my life) were not good examples for my siblings or me, much less consistent providers for my mother.

One of my mothers' husbands kept talking about his ex-wife non-stop, how he missed her and such. When my mom wanted to rearrange the cupboards and set up the kitchen the way she liked it, he said, "No. Keep everything the way Mary Alice put it." When this guy came home from work, he'd go out and check to see if there were tire tracks out in the yard. He wanted to see if my mom had had any visitors. Even back then, I could see that he was trying to control her.

My mom also managed to keep one steady boyfriend. Besides knowing that he was already married, I didn't know a whole lot about Len. He was a character who faded in and out of our lives throughout the years, mostly between her other marriages and casual relationships. I believe he treated her well and didn't mistreat us. Well, not exactly. I suppose now I see that his lack of commitment to my mother was a mistreatment in a way. He just reaffirmed our view that we weren't worth committing to. It's not like we kids ever had anything to say about my mother's relationships. I mean, what kid does with their parents? We just had to tag along, make do, and above all, follow the rule of not talking about *anything* significant. We buried the secrets—and for the longest time, I thought the secrets would bury us.

By age 13, I had my first real boyfriend. That relationship didn't last long though. After him, there was a long list of all the guys that I dated or slept with. I suppose I was following in my mother's footsteps, which I hated, but you need to understand that I didn't like myself. I sought affirmation in others. That meant giving the boys what I thought they wanted. If a boy ended up being a good guy (one who wasn't as wild as me), I would do something to break up with him, because I didn't want anyone to hurt me. I couldn't get close to anyone, because I couldn't even get close to myself, emotionally.

After my mother's second divorce, I think she was still seeing Len off and on. I know she was dating different guys because one was the fourth-grade teacher at the school I was going to. I was so glad I was not in fourth-grade at that time! One guy she once brought home I thought looked really young. He was a pilot. I went up to him and I said, "Do you know how old my mom is?" My mom was, I think, 42 at the time, which I thought was ancient. I couldn't see how she could be dating that young guy. But Mom had lots of relationships. It was hard for me to find out where I fit in.

When my mom was married to her third husband, Ed, we lived in Cherry, Minnesota. Ed had a teenage daughter, Laura, who lived at home with us. My sister Peg and I didn't get along with Laura. I think she didn't want to share her dad with us, even though we didn't really want him for ourselves, anyway. I was 15, Peg was 13, and Laura was 17—three teenage girls thrown together. Laura often would invite her friends over, and they'd smoke pot together. One day I went outside and Laura followed me and said, "Did you tell my dad I was smoking pot?" I told her no, I didn't tell her dad anything. But then she pulled out a knife. She began threatening me. I think she just wanted to scare me.

When things began to worsen between my mom and Ed, Mom decided she would break it all off. *Literally.* Here's what I mean: when we had first moved in with Ed and his daughter, my mother had moved her trailer next to Ed's house. Ed decided that he wanted the trailer to become a part of his house. So he cut a hole in the side of his home and slid Mom's trailer right up to it to join them together. One day, when Mom decided she had enough of Ed and his crazy daughter she said, "Yeah ... that's it. We're outta here." She had someone lined up to hook up the trailer to the back of a truck. A gaping hole stood on the side of it! I saw it myself after we had moved. I'm not sure how long he left it like that, but he eventually patched it up.

Leaving Ed and Laura didn't mean that I wouldn't see them again. No. Months after Laura threatened me with a knife and mom left a hole in Ed's house, we were living in Palo, not far from where we just left. Through the years, I had to follow my mom as she drifted from husband to boyfriend to the next husband. Likewise, I drifted from one boy to the next throughout my school years. Some boys were nice, but those relationships didn't last. Some, not so nice. One incident I remember particularly well.

One day we decided to attend the annual dance back in Cherry at the fairgrounds. In fact, it seems like I remember that my mother went with Ed to this dance, even after they had split. Ed was a constable in Cherry. One duty for the constable is to be a chaperone at the dance. Peg and I were with some older boys. I must have been almost 16. All of us were really drunk. Then the boyfriend of my former step-sister Laura showed up. His name was Mark. He approached me when I was off by myself and said, "Hey, I'm gonna run into Eveleth and go pick Laura up and bring her to the dance. You wanna ride with?"

I didn't know what to think because I didn't think Laura liked me very much. But then Mark told me, "She's been talking about you a lot lately, you know. She's been wondering how you're doing." My faulty logic twisted the message around in my head because I always wanted to make things right with everybody. I believed that things could work out between people, no matter what happened in the past.

So I got into a van with Mark and his friends and we drove to Eveleth. We dropped his friends off, and then the plan was to go to Laura's. But when we got to her house he didn't stop. He said, "Oh, well. I don't think she's home." I thought we'd turn around and head back to the dance. Instead, he turned the car down a gravel road. Then he told me he wasn't going to leave unless I had sex with him. But I wanted no part of it.

"Well, okay. You can just get out the van right here. No problem."

I had no idea where we were. It was dark. I was drunk. So I did what I had to do. After, I told him if he would bring me to my friend Shirley's house, that I wouldn't report him to the cops. He drove me to my friend's house. I hadn't ever been to my friend Shirley's house in the dark. When he brought me down a driveway, I told him that I didn't want him leaving until I knew for sure it was Shirley's place. The moment I stepped out of the car, Mark gunned it in reverse and left me alone. I wasn't even sure whose house it was I was at.

Thankfully, it was the right place. Shirley was surprised that I showed up at her house unannounced. I hadn't called the police or told anyone what had just happened. I was obviously still drunk and they told me to lie down on the couch and sleep it off. The next day I went home and my mom grounded me because I stayed out all night. I didn't tell her what had happened. Sometime shortly after, my sister Peggy decided to run away from home. She and a neighbor girl headed to California; they got rides from truckers.

Much later, when I was older, my mother told me a story.

She said that I had been sleepwalking while she was sitting in the living room. It must have been a few months after the incident with Mark. Recounting the story, she said I walked into the living room and told her about the first time I'd ever slept with anybody. That was a boy named Kevin. I guess I also told her about Mark raping me. I have no memory of it. She said, "Yeah. You told me the whole story the night you were sleepwalking." You think she said anything to me about it the next day after I had admitted everything in my sleep?

Nope. That was her secret to keep.

If I would have graduated from high school, it would have been in '79, but I dropped out in 11th grade. I had met a young man, Mick, and I was in love. I dreamt that my life might become better. It did, but not because I attached myself to Mick. I was pregnant with my first son, Mike, and I was only 16. I never got married to Mick. Instead, I had my son on my own. Mick and I never even moved into together. I met him when my sister and I wanted to take a quick trip over to Virginia, Minnesota, and we decided to hitchhike. Mick and his cousin picked us up. After we got to know each other, we started dating. He was a good nine years older than I was. My mom really liked Mick, because he was mature, he had a house, a job, and he'd been in and out of the Navy. With all the good attributes lined up, the age difference between us didn't matter to her. To her, Mick was good news, a real catch!

When I was pregnant with Mike, Mom, Peggy, and I were living in Biwabik again, next to my grandparents. My older brother Steve had moved out after he graduated from high school, and after Dawn and Wendy had already left home. Steve moved to Chicago and joined a Hindu religious order. He had always been a searcher. Mick and I had split up before he even knew I was pregnant. After I discovered I was pregnant, I wasn't going to tell him. When I gave birth, social services informed me they needed the father's information. I tried to get a hold of Mick, and he said no way, the baby wasn't his. I fought it in court before he finally gave in and signed the paternity papers. My son was almost three years old when his dad decided to do the right thing. Mick made every child support payment, and his family actually treated me with respect and kindness. To me, it's just one of those times where God places good people in a tough situation.

When Mike was a baby, many of my friends from school weren't allowed to hang out with me anymore, because I was a "bad influence." Still, not everyone was that way. One of my girlfriends, Jean Carlson, hadn't been very close to me before I had Mike. After, her family began taking an interest in me. They gave me a Bible and brought me to their Covenant church. It took me a long time to decide that religion was something I wanted to keep pursuing. First, I went to Jean's church when Mike was still a newborn baby. A bit later, I started going to a Unitarian church in Virginia. Their understanding of the world seemed a better fit for me than the Covenant church, which was much more strict. I thought that rules were fine, but without a forgiving God, what good are the rules? If life is just about rules, then we're all sunk. I knew that too well.

When you move around a lot, it's really hard to develop friendships, especially when you're a teenage mother. I had a friend in Biwabik who was a year behind me in school, Elaine. She remained my friend through all the craziness. Today, we're still friends, although we don't see each other often. Her family became Mormon while I was in high school. Elaine's mom just passed away recently. Her parents, they were a big part of my life growing up. Their family was so nice and normal! I just loved to go their place, because they were kind and didn't judge me. It still surprises me today how strict Elaine's parents were with her back then. Once Elaine graduated from high school, she went a bit wild, I think, because of that!

Other than the few good experiences I had with my friends' families, I didn't have any other religious or spiritual upbringing to speak of. Still, I believed in God. I believed in the power of evil, too. But I also believed that good must be more powerful than evil. After I lost my sister Linda, I just couldn't believe I would never see her again. I thought that there had to be something above and beyond, because my life was pretty scary most of the time. Even though I had begun to search for God, bad things kept happening too. I still kept the secrets, but I believe that the ironclad jar of secrets I held so closely was beginning to crack because I started to open up, little by little.

When I was 22, I lived alone in an apartment with Mike, who had grown into a busy preschooler. My mother's fourth husband, Bill, came to my apartment one evening. He was drunk. He started to make advances toward me. Then, he pinned me against my cupboards in the kitchen and began kissing and grabbing me. I pushed him away, cussed at him, and sent him out the door. I told him to never come back. When I told my mom what had happened, she responded in her typical fashion. She said, "Well, what do you expect? You let him buy you a drink at the bar the other night!" Mom did eventually divorce Bill because he had been discovered molesting my niece.

After Mom discovered Bill's molestation of my niece, she said she told the authorities in Biwabik what he had done. But she said they didn't believe her. My sister Wendy said she didn't want to press charges because she didn't want her daughter to have to go through anything. Wendy packed up and moved to a different town. Bill never received justice for his crimes. But my mom, just this once, showed me that a person doesn't have to keep secrets, even though in this case it didn't turn out for the best. (I have since had conversations with my family about my mother's claim. Since we had such a lack of trust in other things she's told us, it's doubtful she ever did any of this.)

With all that's happened in my life, I've thought long and hard why I don't harbor resentments for everything. For me, the painful past is still the past. (And there is still more pain to come!) I think the change began when I really started considering what happens after we die. I thought about Linda and how she didn't deserve to die. I thought of all the terrible and unfair things that happened to me. The only thing that makes a difference for me is that God doesn't forget the past but still sees a greater future for us all. That's my hope, anyway.

After her divorce with Bill, my mother finally married someone who treated her with respect. Keith is my step dad. He's "Papa" Keith and lives in Duluth. I bring my grandchildren today to visit him, knowing that they won't ever have to live in fear of him. I guess Mom saved the best for last. But it would take me a while before I'd meet my best.

In 1988, I got married. Dorian and I had a relationship that was wild, like black magic. When things were good, they were really good. We would complete each other's thoughts and sentences. But when things were bad, they were exceptionally bad. I had gotten pregnant, and Dorian and I got married when our daughter Heather was three months old. Dorian was not only an alcoholic, but he also suffered from mental health issues.

Our relationship was rocky and unhealthy. I know this now. I had told him if he ever hit me that I would leave him. It would only happen once. Then it happened. I ended up giving him a second chance. I knew when he drank and didn't take his meds he was a different person. I couldn't see that I was enabling him. I think I found someone who was at the same level of dysfunction I was.

When Heather was five, the family decided that we needed to do something to help Dorian. He had been depressed and was telling me that he wanted to end it all by wrapping his car around a light pole. Right before Christmas, his brother and I brought him to be evaluated. The doctor took us outside the room. He told us, "You don't need to worry about committing him because I'm taking that decision out of your hands." I was relieved that someone else could decide. After a two-week stay, the hospital let him out. In February, he was starting to feel better and seemed more active and social. *Maybe he's finally okay*, I thought.

On the morning of February 10th, he asked me, "Are you gonna go visit your friend today?" I said, "Yeah." And he said, "Leave me the grocery list. I'll go to the store and pick up what we need." I went to visit my friend and came home. Dorian hadn't returned yet.

I happened to look out the window toward the hospital across the park (we lived only a few blocks away) and I saw a truck that looked an awful lot like ours. But I didn't think anything about it because I believed he would be coming home soon from the grocery store. I thought it was just coincidence that the truck looked like ours.

I know now that instead of going shopping, he drove to a campsite we loved, a place where we had camped for one of our anniversaries. There he had shot himself in the chest with a .44 magnum. The campsite was about one mile back in the woods. Well, he must have panicked, knowing he wasn't going make it unless he could get a ride into town. So after he shot himself and was bleeding all over, he hiked back to the main road to flag a car down and tell the people what he had done. (He must have figured he was too faint to drive.) At first, the people didn't believe him. So he held up his shirt and showed them the hole. One of the guys drove our truck back to the hospital, while the other took Dorian directly to the ER.

Amazingly, he survived. After he stabilized and hospital staff took him off the ventilator, he told me he was sorry that he couldn't even kill himself the right way. His doctor told us that it had been fortunate that he hadn't taken us with him, because he was very paranoid and might have harmed us as well. Later, he was diagnosed with schizophrenia.

After he recuperated and returned home, he started getting scary, threatening the kids and me. I finally had enough and left him. I hadn't yet divorced him. Six months later, he ended up getting in a drunk driving accident that killed one of his friends in a car ahead of him. That sent him to prison for vehicular manslaughter. I thought, *I'm not going to kick him when he's down and divorce him now.* When he got out of jail in '95, we talked a couple of times about getting back together, but I decided I couldn't live with the drama anymore. After the divorce was final in March, Dorian called to tell me he had seen a psychic, who had told him that he and I would get back together within ten years. I knew he had completely gone off the deep end. Dorian took his own life about five years later.

Just recently, my daughter Heather lent me the journal Dorian kept while he was in treatment. In it, he wrote that he had asked God why he suffered from depression and suicidal ideation. He also wrote that maybe he wasn't receptive to God's help until he had taken the desperate act of trying to kill himself. He wrote that he knew that Jesus must have carried him out of the woods that day so he could discover just how sick he was. He really opened up in the journal, sharing how thankful he was that God had taught him so much about himself in treatment. I guess it shows me how God was trying to work in Dorian's life, too. It's hard for all of us, but it must have been doubly so for Dorian.

Mick's parents (the grandparents of my first child, Mike) had always treated me with respect, his mom especially. I've always believed a person can't have too many other mothers, and she was one of the people I considered "mom." Shortly after I left Dorian, Mick's father Marvin invited me to go camping on Isle Royale in Lake Superior. Mick's friend Craig also came along for the trip. After two or three days in the wilderness, Craig and I hit it off so well, that we talked about seeing each other again. At the time, Craig was living in Hazen, North Dakota, and worked at a power plant. When he got back home, he called to tell me that he wanted me to come live with him, that he felt lost without me.

I told him that I couldn't leave Minnesota without the two of us marrying because I thought Dorian (who hadn't yet taken his life) might cause trouble. I didn't want to put Heather in a difficult situation either. Three weeks after our camping trip, we were married. That's how long it took for the marriage license to come through. I called my pastor in Ely and said, "Pastor Bill, I need you to do a wedding."

He asked, "Who's getting married?" And I said, "I am."

He said, "I didn't know you were dating anybody."

I said, "I'm not!"

Craig had never been married and was nervous I was going to change my mind. I wasn't though. Soon we had an official ceremony in Minnesota. Mick, the father of my son and Craig's friend, was the best man at our wedding. Like my mom always said, everything in life tends to come full circle.

No doubt, it was an impulsive decision and one that in most cases would turn out for the worst. Still, Craig and I decided this was something that we wanted to do. We both felt there was a reason we were supposed to be together. We just went for it. All my friends thought I was nuts. I probably was! But I don't think it was luck; I believe it was God's hand working in my life. Craig was a wonderful husband and my very best friend. I was finally very happy. At the same time, I was also terrified. I kept wondering when the other shoe would drop, that a good relationship couldn't ever last. Part of me felt like running away, much like I had done as a teenager when I would meet a boy who treated me decently.

I realized that unless I made an effort to live life differently, it would be awfully easy to fall into the same pattern as what I'd become used to. Ever since I got pregnant with Mike, I promised myself that my kids were going to have a different life than I had. I had good intentions with Mick, Dorian, with boyfriends where I tried to make a run at it, but I failed. I don't regret marrying Dorian or having Mike when I was young. In some ways, I think being a teenage mother probably saved me from a lot worse—from drinking and drugs, because honestly, I was still attracted to the dark side. Craig was the exact opposite, though. He was stable, loving, empathetic, and loved me. Sometimes you have to grow up, right? I'm glad God brought Craig and me together. I am who I am because of my past, for better or worse.

After we had lived (happily) in North Dakota for about a decade, we decided that we wanted to move back to Minnesota. Craig would be retiring soon, and we wanted our own place, a home where we could build fresh memories together and where we could be closer to family. In North Dakota, we lived in a house that everyone called "the old Mannie place." The home took on the name of its previous owner, even after they were long gone. Craig and wanted to have a place of our own, "the Fallgren place," a home that would always have our name. It is where I live right now in Minnesota. I was back home, but this time it was *my* home. I moved into the brand-new home right away, and my daughter Heather moved home four months after. Craig was still working in North Dakota after we bought the house. When he finished at his job, he moved in. At last, life seemed like it was finally going well.

Then during the Christmas of 2014, Craig complained he didn't have any energy and felt weak. He didn't want to go to the doctor because he knew they were going to tell him to lose weight, to get more exercise, or maybe that he'd need a stent in his heart. He told me he didn't need to pay anyone to tell him what he already knew. However, it got to the point where he couldn't walk up the stairs without getting winded. Finally, he agreed to go to the local clinic and get some blood work done.

He went to the clinic at two o'clock in the afternoon. At nine o'clock that evening, we got a call from the doctor. The doctor wanted Craig to head immediately to the emergency room because they needed to re-run some of the tests. They confirmed the results from the first tests: his red cell count, white cells, platelets… everything had bottomed out. The next day, they told us he had acute myeloid leukemia.

The doctor recommended we go to St. Mary's Hospital in Duluth, Minnesota, a larger city. The drive to Duluth was very emotional for me. I kept saying, *No, they must have misdiagnosed you. This can't be happening. I don't want this to happen! Please, God, no!*

When we got to Duluth, he began chemo immediately, because the cancer had already progressed so far. The doctors there told us how seriously ill he was, that he didn't have much of a chance because his type of leukemia was adversely affected by his genetics. Craig did chemo for thirty days in Duluth. The specialists suggested we go to Mayo Clinic in Rochester. Until meeting with the doctors at the Mayo Clinic, we didn't get the full picture of how seriously ill he was. But, we had a bit of hope—we learned that if Craig received stem-cell therapy from bone marrow, he might have a chance. Craig's sister turned out to be a perfect match.

His sister agreed to go through with the transplant. It was also very emotionally draining for her. She loved her brother dearly. Our world had been turned upside down. But isn't that how life is? Just a second is all it takes, and things will never be the same. Right after the transplant, things got difficult. Then he seemed to turn the corner and got better. For a while, we thought he might pull through. In the end, the cancer ate away at his body. He didn't look anything like the healthy, full-bodied man that I knew.

I'm thankful that Craig got to live the dream he had been looking forward to. He hoped that he would be well enough to walk down the aisle with my daughter, Heather, at her wedding, which was in February of 2016. Craig told everyone, "When Heather gets married, I'm gonna walk her down that aisle. Just stay outta my way!" He got his wish. I think that's what he was living for. After the wedding, his health deteriorated quickly. Craig died on March 8, 2016.

From the beginning, I think Craig didn't really connect with how sick he was. It took him until October in 2015 when he shared with me that for the first time he was afraid. Up to that point, he tried to console me, telling me that everything would work out, that things weren't as bad as they seem. I think it was his way of protecting my feelings. But he never asked, "Why me?" We knew there is no answer for that question.

I believe strongly that God doesn't make bad things happen to people. Throughout my life, and even more so after I met Craig, I have come to believe that God places people in your life when and where God knows you need them. The bad things? I don't know why they happen. All I know is that we are meant to be there for each other. Some days I don't want to get up. It's been seven months now, and some days are just hard. Just recently, I went to Craig's family reunion at the farm. Craig got his family to start meeting every year. I feel a part of that family still, but it was just so hard to be there without him.

In September of 2008, long before my husband Craig's diagnosis, my mom discovered her breast cancer had returned. The doctors said she only had a short time to live. Although she didn't visit us in our new home often, Mom especially loved one room in our house with a large picture window overlooking my small garden. In fact, when she first entered that room after Craig and I had bought the house, she said, "This is where you're supposed to be." My mom was right: everything comes full circle. I spent many hours visiting my mother and my step-dad Keith at their place before she died.

For a long time, I was more upset at my mother than I was with my dad and all the chaos and abuse. My dad had grown up in a terrible environment; he had a horrendous life as a kid. Both his parents were alcoholics, and they beat and yelled at him. From what he shared with me, he basically grew up in a bar. Incest was also an issue in their family. Later in my life, I had reconnected with my father and had forgiven him. We had reestablished a connection and he had quit drinking. I believe he felt bad for the choices he had made. Actually, when my dad didn't drink, he was a decent person; I could talk with him without being afraid. We were able to talk things through, to expose the secrets we had once kept and let them wither in the light. Conversations with my mother were never as forthcoming. With her, when I asked her about what had happened in the past, she always blew things off or minimized them. She said, "It doesn't do any good to hold on to the past." I believe my mom didn't want to face the past with all its ugliness because it was too painful.

Before my mother died, I was able to make peace with her as well, despite her unwillingness to uncover our family secrets. My husband Craig had said she was only doing her best with what she was given, and I suppose that's true. However, I think the change I had made with myself—that I no longer let the past define me, even though I won't deny it—allowed me to let my mother be who she was. I didn't need to change her to love her. In the end, it's about the love we have for each other in the moment that counts. I know my mom loved me. Now, remembering the days we spent together when she was dying—I think those are some of the most precious moments I ever spent with her.

There's another incident comes to mind. After her diagnosis but before she got very ill, I was visiting her at her home. She asked me to go on a walk with her in her garden. The routine of watering the plants and rooting out weeds was her daily act of "surveying her kingdom." Her garden was huge, and she had a wide variety of plants and beautiful flowers. Even in her house, African violets and tropical plants sat in nearly every window. One particular bed of flowers she took great pride in—her tiger lilies. She loved them because they were not only beautiful but also hardy. "They're just like me," she said.

While we were walking outside that day, she told me, "Here's where I keep this plant, and this is what you need to do to keep it healthy. And these plants over by the shed, you can't overwater." She was very specific about how each set of plants needed tending. She said, "You're going to need to know this stuff so you can take care of my plants when I'm not here anymore." I told her I would do my best, and of course that I would keep after my step-father, Keith, to do his part in tending the garden when I wasn't there.

After my mom died, I regret to say that I did not keep my promise to tend the garden as she would have liked. I don't know if it would have mattered, though, because Keith ended up taking out a lot of the plants to make it easier for him to maintain. He even ended up throwing away the African violets she was so proud to have grown indoors in northern Minnesota. The other gardens that he didn't tear out became choked with weeds. But the tiger lilies continue to bloom, year after year, despite her daughter or husband's lack of a green thumb.

They remain as stunningly beautiful and hardy as the day she first planted them.

Maybe there is a lesson to learn from those lilies. No matter how choked my life became with the weeds of pain, loss, difficulty, or stress, the gift is in knowing where I am rooted. For me, my roots are planted in my identity as a forgiven a child of God. My faith keeps me going and urges me to get out of bed for the day, even when I've lost the people who I most loved: my sister Linda, my mother, my best friend and husband, Craig. I know that I need to pass on my love to my grandchildren, so that they know that they, too, are rooted in the love and grace of God.

I interviewed Kitty in one four-hour visit. While I was writing, I had follow-up questions, so we communicated again on the phone and through email. My questions dealt primarily with Kitty's spiritual upbringing. I was interested in how she became a person of deep faith and a devoted follower of Jesus. Today, Kitty belongs to an Evangelical Lutheran Church in America congregation near her home.

Because her parents had not provided a formal background for her religious beliefs, I asked her where she believed her spiritual grounding came from.

She said, "Well, I'm not sure. It's hard to remember back that far. But I really started to think about what happens after we die after my sister Linda was murdered. I believed there just has to be something more. And I don't know where I got this from—it just came to me—but I always had the feeling that Linda was protecting me. She was taking care of me, you know. And even after ... my parents were divorced, I still felt like Linda was protecting me. I think she's my angel. It was ... just a feeling I got. That was God. I know it. Even before

I knew what it was, I think that feeling deep inside was God working in my life.

"I don't know why I believed this. I thought there had to be a reason that God made Linda and me sisters. I also believed— still do—that God didn't cause Linda to be murdered. But you know, there's a reason why I am who I am, and a reason that I was born into my family. I think it was a belief system I grew into. But, really, I probably got things figured out when my sister died and I was seeing a counselor because I was so angry all the time. That was when Mike was small, and I mean, there were a lot of times when I was mad, and I was yelling and you know, throwing things around the house *(laughs)*. I think for the first two years after he was born, I think I felt more like I was babysitting. I kept waiting for somebody to come pick this kid up."

I was interested that Kitty had received counseling and asked her to say more about her experience with the counseling sessions.

"It helped me work through my anger issues. And [the counselor] helped me see that I was a mother for Mike. But, honestly, I still had questions after I was finished," she said.

"I've always been a searcher. I wanted to know if there was something more to life than the pain or fear I felt. And I wanted to know if Linda still existed in some way. I guess at first it was for selfish reasons," she said and laughed.

"What do you mean by 'selfish'?"

"I dunno. I think at first I just needed to know if Linda was still with me somehow. But don't misunderstand; I really think that was just the beginning. God meets you where you are and goes from there. But I think your beliefs aren't created without other people helping you along the way. I belonged to lots of different churches."

Our conversation gravitated toward her specific experiences she had had with different faith communities. She had already shared with me that some families had reached out to her when she became a teenage mother. I wanted to know what other people or congregations had done to shape her beliefs.

She said, "I kept looking, for sure. I didn't give up... I ended up being a Mormon for a short period of time when I was 21. Yeah, and it took a long time to get out too," she added, laughing. "They first showed up at my door. They said, 'We gotta get you baptized.' I was unsure at first: I thought I should probably wait a little bit and make sure I know what I want to do. But they had me look things up in the Bible, and I knew where to find everything because I'm a reader. They kept coming back and told me it would be a good thing for me to join their church. Well, you wanna know what? I didn't really want to! I still did, though.

"My childhood friend Elaine, you see, her parents had ended up joining the Mormon church. Elaine never became a Mormon. But they encouraged me to keep at it, to keep studying. In fact, Elaine's dad is the one who baptized me. I guess they convinced me to do it. So there I was, a Mormon. But I didn't like it. And they wouldn't let me out of the church."

Kitty went into what she believed was the rationale for their actions. She said, "I suppose they feel they have a responsibility to care for you. Every week they would show up at my door and they'd haul me into church. At first, I went, but then I said, 'I'm not going.' They told me the only way that I could get out is they have their own little court system thing when the council meets with you and you discuss all this stuff. So I dressed in the most hippyish clothes I could find. I went in there and told them my story and about what my life was like, and they decided it was better to excommunicate me and I was finally out. Nobody showed up at my door anymore!"

Since I had not heard about the process that Mormons went through to excommunicate their members (at least in northern Minnesota in the early 80s), I found her story both humorous and interesting—she certainly knew what would turn them off and shoo them away. I wondered what she learned, if anything, from that experience.

She said, "I think I learned I didn't want to be a Mormon!"

I asked her to say more.

She paused, and then said, "Um, I also think God was telling me that it was okay to be me, that I could be the person God made me to be without believing a bunch of silly stuff."

I asked her, "What happened after that? Did you join other churches?"

She said, "Oh yeah. Lots of them. After I got out of the Mormon Church, then... I was back in Virginia, Minnesota. I didn't go to church for a while there. And then, um, yeah, it was after Heather was born that I really got to church again. That was when I was married to Dorian. And ... yeah, I was struggling."

I said, "No doubt. But how did belonging to a faith community make a difference to you?"

She said, "Oh, it was tough there, too. That was at a Lutheran church in Embarrass, Minnesota. I liked it lots, but the pastor ended up molesting several of the kids. Ended up having to leave the church. Yeah, turned out that bad things were happening there."

It was all I could do to keep myself from chuckling too much at the irony of that pastor's missteps in a community named *Embarrass*.

Kitty continued, "But, Dorian's sister-in-law Melinda and I became very close. And so I just started attending church with her. I joined by the time Heather was two. I was teaching Sunday school and everything. It was a whole different life than the Mormons. Much better for me. I think that place formed my faith a lot. I liked what they believed about grace. That God is a God of grace, not judgment."

Kitty continued sharing how her faith life had evolved, both through the relationships she had made, but also through her understanding how God had been present with her through the difficult periods of her life.

"It's like I was seeing for the first time that things are not always what they seem. It taught me to look under the surface of everything. It's just like faith: you feel it in here *(points to heart)*. It's like you finally recognize that God's been with you all along through your life. I was never alone. There was always someone looking out for me. I did go through a stage where I thought this religion stuff is crazy."

I asked her what she meant.

"Well, *Religion does seem crazy* in some ways if you're on the outside looking in. I mean, it's like these people are all nuts! But it speaks to me somehow. And I keep coming back because it's doing something for me. I believe that God is working through me. I grew a lot during that time.

I wanted to know more. I asked her, "How did belonging to a church—or your spiritual growth during that time—make a difference to you then?"

She smiled at me and said, "Oh. Loads. When Dorian was so sick, but before he shot himself, I remember the doctors had told me that if things turned for the worse that I should call them. So one night I was just waiting for him to fall asleep, because he was so paranoid and so jumpy."

I could see that sharing this part of the story was difficult for her because she struggled to communicate through her tears.

"I thought if I tried to call the hospital, he might come out yelling, and he'd grab the phone and rip it out of the wall, because he kept telling me he's fine, that he's not sick. I remember looking up at the ceiling and praying, 'Dear God, make me crazy. Please make me crazy! Because I can't deal with this anymore.' I was so knocked down. I didn't feel any lighting bolts come out of the sky. And I didn't go crazy *(laughs)*.

"When I look back on it now, I know God gave me the

strength to pull through. I just know it. My church helped me too. I think I felt God's strength helping me. So, God seems to have worked in the present and the future. In fact, when I got out to North Dakota and Craig and I were together, it was the first time that I felt so healthy and so happy. But I got [depressed] and fell apart! Craig said, 'Well, it's because now you can finally let all that go. You're finally able to work through this stuff.'

"I really believe that God's everywhere, and has been all throughout my life. Even now, Craig's gone, but he's still is taking care of me too. I guess now he and Linda can divvy up the job watching over me," she said, laughing.

"I don't give up. It's not an option for me. You know, when people tell me, 'Oh, I don't know how you could go through this or that. I could never do it.' Well, yeah you could. You know, any of us can. It's when you look back that you see what you've come through that you know God was there."

Kitty leaned in; she was obviously passionate about her beliefs. She said, "At the time you don't know if you can get through those times … you're just putting one foot in front of the other. Also, I want to say that for Craig, it settled him to know that my church family would keep taking care of me. He told me he knew he wasn't gonna have to worry about me after he was gone."

I asked Kitty whether she believed that faith is the spiritual asset that has given her the resilience she's seemed to have through the difficult times in her life.

"Yeah," she said, nodding, "faith is an asset. Maybe hope a little bit too with me … because it was always something to hold on to. But I don't think I recognized it at the time; I do now. I'm convinced that after you die nobody's sick, and all the demons people have dealt with, they're all gone, defeated. I used to dream about my sister Linda all the time when I was young. More than once, I woke up in the middle of the night and felt like there was a weight of somebody sitting at the end of my bed, like somebody was sitting there watching over me."

I asked, "Do you think your faith makes you a more resilient person; that you're able to bounce back after the struggles you've gone through?"

"I don't feel resilient. Everybody tells me how resilient I am—how strong or tough I am. I know I'm strong; maybe that's what it means to be resilient!" she chuckled, adding, "I know I've been through a lot of stuff, and I think that's prepared me for the next bunch of stuff that has come up, because my whole life there have been things going on. I've never missed anybody as much Craig. I've never loved anybody as much as him. When a person considers how our relationship started," she said with a giggle, "the only answer for it is it was a *gift from God* for both of us to be together. There were so many things I didn't think I could have ever dealt with unless Craig and I were together, like when Dorian committed suicide."

I asked, "How do you go on today?"

She said, "I just started doing volunteer work, and I've had one day at the Common Good in town. I never worked much because of health problems with my neck. I have always been the one in my family with health issues ... from the time I was born and still continuing now. I have diagnoses of mixed connective-tissue disease, rheumatoid arthritis, fibromyalgia, degenerative disc disease, hypothyroid, chronic kidney disease, high blood pressure, sleep apnea, migraines, plus a few surgeries—spinal fusion, full hysterectomy, gall bladder, sinus surgery.

"I also believe that some of these health issues are directly related to the trauma and stresses. In our family, we didn't talk about the past. We kept secrets. I raised my kids in a different way; I did not want them to have the kind of upbringing that my siblings and I had. Life comes around full circle, but it's okay to break the cycles that are unhealthy. I'm going to try and help out where I can, when I can. Life is still good. I will stay in this house until I die. To me, life is about connecting with people and doing our best to help each other."

Resilience and Faith

One of the few passages of scripture I have memorized comes from the New Testament Epistle to the Hebrews: "Now faith is the assurance of things hoped for, the conviction of things not seen."[24] Maybe I continue to remember it because it gives us such a clear-cut definition. In this light, I find it fascinating that Kitty herself connected faith and hope to her life story and to her ability to be resilient: "Yeah. Faith is an asset. Maybe hope a little bit, too, with me… because it was always something to hold on to."

In Hebrews, the writer describes faith as a common trait that believers in the present world could connect with those in the past. The author of the letter (and, really, Hebrews is primarily a speech of encouragement) calls a questioning community to find solace that Jesus was indeed the promised Messiah.

It's easy to cherry-pick passages from scripture and use them for your own purposes, without considering a verse's original context. However, it seems that the passage is just as relevant today as it was when the author penned it nearly 2000 years ago. Faith is still about believing (and hoping) in (and for) something, even though there may be no physical proof to back that belief up. Kitty believes in a loving, graceful God who is the creator, savior, and sustainer of the world. And she believes that despite the terrible circumstances she lived through. Another person living a life similar to Kitty's could easily deny the existence of God—or at the least a graceful, loving God.

---

[24] Heb. 11:1 NRSV

Kitty continues to believe. Actually, she believes *all the more* in a God who loves her—despite her abuse, rape, becoming a mother early in life, living through Dorian's suicide, and losing her mother and her husband Craig to cancer. Why? We could say that she's delusional, that she believes in something imaginary. Certainly, this would be a completely rational argument, but I don't believe that explanation either. Maybe I'm delusional too, but it doesn't take into account the billions of people on the planet who have similar beliefs. I think Kitty has faith in God because it is what God has gifted to her. Her faith serves a purpose: it gives her the hope and trust in a power greater than herself. Faith is the hope that life, after all, isn't completely falling apart at the seams or taking a nose-dive into a meaningless abyss.

Besides, Kitty does have proof. She only received it *after the fact*. Looking back, Kitty sees the events in her life when she should have fallen apart emotionally, but didn't. (She reported that she did also struggle physically with the ailments she believes she suffered because of the stress.) Still, she held on to the belief that God was there for her, not only in the people who God placed in her path, but in the faith that God would work everything out—even if everything didn't work out in the short term.

C. S. Lewis, the fantasy novelist and Christian apologist, wrote, "I believe in Christianity as I believe that the Sun has risen not only because I see it, but because by it I see everything else."[25] For certain, his argument is circular. Just the same, faith by its very nature of hoping for that we cannot see is a circular reasoning! We can easily boil faith down into a rationalized pragmatism. That is to say, faith becomes a simple byproduct

---

[25] Lewis, C.S. 1962. ""They Asked for a Paper." In *Is Theology Poetry?*, by C.S. Lewis. 164-165. London: Geoffrey Bless.

of the imagination to make the nihilism of life more bearable. However, for Kitty—and me too—it's more complex than that. We believe, because to do otherwise isn't who we are. Lack of faith isn't in our character. The benefits to faith—if you can call them that—only come as a result of belief, but aren't a source of that faith itself. For Kitty and me, we believe because it's who we are. The act of faith is to trust, to act not knowing the outcome. To grow in faith is to make those actions as best we can without knowing the end results.

If spiritual assets bring us closer to our Higher Power, we do not face life's difficulties alone. Those assets allow us to find a greater purpose and meaning within the stress. Faith certainly qualifies as a spiritual asset for Kitty, because her belief and hope in that which she could not see allowed her (paradoxically) to see more clearly, love more deeply, and act more courageously in spite of the horrible circumstances she found herself in. Faith got her through, even when she didn't think she could do so under her own power.

Since Kitty could not change many of the circumstances in her life, they ended up changing her, instead. She made decisions—for better or worse—about what direction to go based on the firm foundation of faith. She believed that she would continue to be God's beloved daughter, no matter what happened. Just as I've had to learn to live *into* my story of addiction and recovery, Kitty knew that her story wasn't supposed to end yet, even when things looked bleak. I believe strongly that faith is more than simply "blind faith." Instead, it is knowing that a loving power greater than yourself is leading you forward, through the pain, the fear, and the sadness to something better. Faith is the assurance of things hoped for; it is the hope that drives us to move forward to live for a better day.

Chapter Five

Forgiveness

The first month I was in treatment for addiction to alcohol and drugs at Hazelden in Center City, Minnesota, one concept about Twelve Step recovery I couldn't seem to wrap my mind around: resentment.

"Resentments? I don't have any resentments," I told my counselor and my peers. They weren't buying it. Everyone's been hurt. Everyone experiences different degrees of anger or annoyance or loss. Some face trauma. The human condition dictates that pain is part of the equation of life. There is a reason why Twelve Step recovery deals with resentments head on: an almost certain relapse is built on that seething anger and perceived lack of control. Twelve Step recovery looks to resolve that resentment.

In my case, I discovered the number one resentment I was harboring was with myself. I was angry with myself for having spun a life of lies, a web I had intricately woven so that the strands of fiction and reality were indistinguishable to me. However, being aware of the need for change and integrating it into your life are two separate things. I discovered that in order to be able to tread on the road to honesty, I first had to build a foundation of forgiveness. I needed to forgive myself, both for the harm I had done others, but also for the harm I had brought upon myself. As I share in the introduction, honesty became my spiritual asset to build a more robust resilience to the stress I would no doubt incur simply by being alive.

Later in my recovery, I needed to work through amends with the people I had harmed where it was possible. The action of placing myself at the mercy of others was even more difficult than forgiving myself because it was so wholly different than I had acted in the past. I used to lie and subtly (and sometimes not so delicately) manipulate others to get what I wanted. For the first time in my life, I felt naked without the fine robes and dashing sashes to hide my true self, a self-conscious and fear-driven person, a pink and squishy soul who wanted to be liked, needed, and cared for.

What I learned is most people are willing to forgive if you come to them with honest contrition—the majority of my amends-making were positive experiences. One wasn't, but I ended up learning to let go of the new resentment that could have kept munching away at my serenity. I was able to forgive that person for not forgiving me.

Although I view the world primarily through the lens of Jesus' example of forgiveness, the wisdom of the Buddha places forgiveness in a new light. The Buddha doesn't directly mention forgiveness in the writings from that tradition. Instead, he spoke more about the destructive potential anger has to lay waste to both parties. We can plainly see what he was getting at from these verses from the Dhammapada: "'He abused me, he struck me, he overpowered me, he robbed me.' Those who harbor such thoughts do not still their hatred,"[26] and, "Overcome the angry by non-anger; overcome the wicked by goodness; overcome the miser by generosity; overcome the liar by truth."[27]

Resentment and anger are devastating to a person's resilience

---

[26] Thera, Buddharakkhita. 2003. *The Dhammapada: The Buddha's Path of Wisdom.* Kandy, Sri Lanka: Buddhist Publication Society. 21.
[27] Ibid., 76.

to stress, trauma, and the inevitable disappointments of life. These negative emotions eat at you because the anger simply has nowhere to turn—like a child's pinwheel out in the wind, resentment and anger spin and spin without any resolution. Conversely, forgiveness strengthens a person's resilience. Forgiveness of another (or yourself) isn't weakness; it's an asset and a strength. And it sometimes requires great effort to carry through. The rewards, however, are beautiful.

Pastor Rick Rouse, an ELCA minister and author of the book *Fire of Grace: The Healing Power of Forgiveness28,* intimately knows just how difficult the work behind forgiveness can be, but also how wonderfully freeing and resilience-building it can be to be able to authentically forgive. Rick was serving in a congregation in Washington State when a serial arsonist burned down his church building. His story shows that forgiveness not only began the process of healing, for him and his congregation, but it became the founding moment in his ministry and his life to be resilient to the further loss and stress he would experience.

Rick's Story

I began my ministry at Trinity Lutheran in Lynnwood, Washington, the summer of 1987. This was the place where my life radically shifted (several times), but more importantly where I discovered what forgiveness really looks like.

By the spring of 1992, I'd been at Trinity Lutheran in Lynnwood for five years, and I'd been an ordained minister for

---

28 Rouse, Richard W. 2005. *Fire of Grace: The Healing Power of Forgiveness.* Minneapolis, MN: Augsburg Fortress.

nearly twenty. I attended a clergy support group with a number of fellow colleagues and we had a mentor who was a former Lutheran chaplain. This man suggested that I had entered into a burnout stage with my job and that I needed to think about taking a sabbatical. I took the advice to heart, so I approached my leadership team at Trinity and they agreed that it would be a good idea for me to take a sabbatical. That summer in '92, I took the time off to read, reflect, and basically reconnect with myself and my family. The experience was refreshing and trans-formative— I realized that in my ministry for nearly twenty years, I'd become a human *doing* instead of a human *being*.

However, within two weeks of returning to my call from my sabbatical, I was sitting at home reading, early on a Sunday morning, when I received a phone call at 4 a.m. It was the Lynnwood Fire Chief. He said, "You better get down here right away. Your church is burning down."

Looking back on this event, I seriously believe that in God's providence, God knew that I needed to get myself healed and renewed by taking a sabbatical to come back and face this trauma in a healthy way.

I remember getting down to the church at about probably 6:30 a.m. My congregational president and the custodian were there. The fire crew was hosing the building down because they were concerned that the fire was going to jump from the sanctuary to the custodian's house right next door, to the church building. I stood watching the fire fighters putting out the fire. Ironically, my congregational president was surprised I had come. He said, "What are you doing here, pastor? You're supposed to be on sabbatical!"

I remembered saying something like, "Oh ... I just have to be here! I mean, look at this!"

The church's associate pastor had been on vacation during that time, and we also employed an intern and she was there all by herself. Technically, she was assigned to lead worship that

Sunday. I guess I had automatically stepped back into pastor mode. I needed to help out. I needed to respond, somehow.

We decided that we were going to have worship here that morning, despite the fire. We didn't know how we were going to pull it off—we thought we'd hold it out in the parking lot or something. The way the congregation, the leaders, our intern—everybody—the response was simply amazing. From the time that I went home to shower and returned, one group had shown up with a truckload of folding chairs, somebody else hobbled together a makeshift altar and brought candles, another provided Eucharistic vessels and bread and wine, yet another showed up with a box of hymnals, and someone even set up a portable sound system. By the time I came back from showering, the people had set everything up like we'd been planning this outdoor service for months. It was a minor miracle, a sign from God that the Body of Christ survives despite tragedy.

We didn't yet know the cause of the fire, only that our building was burned to the ground. The church fire had been all over the news and I remember when I went home to shower, I turned on the TV, and of course, it was the main story. For me, when I was there in person, I was still in disbelief, in shock, I suppose. But when I saw it on TV, it became real. Isn't that strange?

The reporters on the TV news were saying that *two* churches had burned that day, early that morning. So when I got back to help lead worship with my intern, the saying also became real that "a church is more than a building." I had to be convicted that the people would come through this challenge. God provided a text from the Old Testament, from the book of the Prophet Isaiah:

When you pass through the waters, I will be with you;
 and through the rivers, they shall not overwhelm you;
when you walk through fire you shall not be burned,

and the flame shall not consume you.[29]

Somehow, that text just came in my head. Our synod's Assistant to the Bishop was there as well, and shared about the resurrection and arising out of the ashes in new life. Obviously, it was a moving experience. Since many had come to worship not knowing that the church had burned down, they were in shock, seeing the smoldering ashes in the background. During worship, our backs were to the building. The firefighters had only just left by the time we began worship. The whole experience was eerie, surreal really.

The next day I met with our leadership team, and of course, everybody was still in shock from the trauma of the fire, still feeling a real sense of loss. I was trying to offer encouragement, but people weren't sure where to turn to next. I suggested we first get in touch with the insurance. People were really great about stepping up. We decided to use the intern's house as a command center as soon as she moved out. (Her term with us was about to come to an end anyway.) We started talking about strategies for how we needed to move forward.

First, though, I need to mention a couple of other significant things that happened. One is that the fire chief who was present on site that Sunday came up to me and said, "You know, I'm the pastor of the Seventh-Day Adventist Church just down the street. I want you to know that our church building is yours for as long as you need it." We had a home for two-and-half years while our building was being rebuilt. It was nice, because Seventh-Day Adventists meet on Saturday, so we were able to continue our Sunday morning schedule just as it had been.

The other point I need to mention is that some in the church were just feeling disheartened by it all. They thought we should disperse to other congregations. But others disagreed and thought we should rebuild. I said, "No, we need to first spend some time

---

[29] Isa. 43:2 NRSV

in prayer and discernment and go through a visioning process to discover what God is calling us to be and to do in this time and place."

The prayer, conversation, and time spent in discernment were important because it got us talking about what it really means to be a congregation of healing and reconciliation after this painful event. The leadership team agreed on a strategy to move forward. We talked about how we were going to initiate a time of healing for the congregation. Together, we set up various "cottage meetings."

First, though, the church leadership confronted me with one unresolved issue—they said, "Pastor, you still have a couple of weeks of your sabbatical left. You need to take it." Their concern choked me up, but it was also one of the hardest things in my life to carry through with. I felt like I had to be there, to be a leader in this difficult time.

In all of this, too, I had experienced loss personally. My office was destroyed. I had stoles that my mother had made for my ordination that went up in flames. Of course, all the books in my library were gone. Beyond the personal loss was the trauma of the congregation itself—we had just recently celebrated our 50th anniversary and launched a new building program for a new addition for our building. Everyone expected before the fire that we were moving forward in a positive direction. To have all of those hopes and dreams destroyed was too much. After all, a building is just a building, but it's more than that, too. People had married there. They buried their loved ones. Babies were baptized. All those memories, gone. They went up in flames.

So you can understand that I, as a leader in this congregation, had a tough time taking the advice of the church leadership that I finish my sabbatical. I needed to *do* something! I needed to be there for them, to comfort and offer guidance during this inconceivable tragedy. However, my congregation was right—they knew better how to be present for me in the way I needed at the time. That's God's work in action through God's people.

One of the aspects about my role as a pastor that I had learned in my sabbatical is that I needed to be able to step back and trust that everything was in good hands and that I didn't have to be the one in control. My parents, my wife, and I had a condo over at Ocean Shores, which is on the coast of Washington. I went over there for a week of personal healing and reflection. One day near the end of our stay, I was out running on the sand dunes. I broke down, just crying and screaming, "God … what the *hell* are you up to?!" The trauma had shifted from denial to anger.

Shortly after, I moved into the bargaining stage. I said, "Okay God, we need to do this and this, and you'll do this other thing. And I guess I can come through it all." I had to learn to completely give things over to God and to my leadership team. Like I mentioned, learning to let go and trust were key points I took away from my sabbatical. Because of the time I'd spent, I was able to come back no longer a burned-out pastor, but instead renewed and refreshed with a different perspective. I was able to be there for my congregation much healthier than I would have been had I not taken the time. I've never forgotten how God conveyed God's wisdom through the people to give me the assets I needed to be a healthy leader.

As it turned out, I would need to be in that place if I were to guide the congregation through the healing and forgiveness we would need to do. At the time, we had signs that arson was suspected, but we didn't know any confirmed details until after I returned from my finished sabbatical.

Part of the challenge for the arson investigators was that the young man who did it didn't use any accelerants like gas or lighter fluid—he simply would go looking for places that were under construction, like our church building had been for the addition we were putting on. Then he would take his Bic lighter and set the construction materials ablaze. As a consequence of the lack of accelerants, it was hard for authorities to initially determine the source of the fire.

Still, it became plain that someone was intentionally setting these fires, because of all the buildings that were going up in flames. Over a period of six months, buildings kept getting torched. People in our town were on edge. Some congregations even kept vigil in their churches to protect them. Everyone wondered who was responsible and all the while we had to move on. We kept holding our cottage meetings to discern the direction God wanted us to go. We also had services of healing. At that time, I don't believe people were thinking about forgiveness because we still didn't know who was responsible. Without a party to blame, who can you forgive? I do believe though that some were angry. How could anyone not be? We had lost so much. People were in pain and needed to first heal before they could move on to the next stage.

One especially touching memory comes to mind. In one of our cottage meetings, people talked about their shared sense of loss and grief. One mother stood up and said, "My little, six-year-old daughter was sitting at the kitchen table and she was coloring an egg carton with red and orange. She started cutting it up in pieces and she told me, 'That's our church.' She was putting flames on it, and then she was cutting it up and it was no longer there; it was destroyed."

Playing "fire" was this little girl's way, a child's way, of dealing with her sense of loss of her Sunday school.

About six months after our building was destroyed, the arson squad informed us that they had arrested someone. He was charged with over 100 counts of intentional arson. He confessed to about 70 of those.

To back up, the authorities had released a composite picture in the newspaper of what the arsonist looked like. This happened all while the other fires were taking place. Someone evidently witnessed him at one of the fires. The composite drawing looked very familiar to me, but I couldn't place it exactly. Then a short time after the arsonist, Paul Keller, was arrested. I suddenly realized that this young man had sat in my office only a few months before the fire. That was probably back in May of '92. Paul's father owned an advertising company and Paul was the primary client representative. When Paul had come to my office, we discussed an advertising campaign for the local Lutheran churches in the area. I was the dean of our conference at the time, and we chatted about the campaign.

Later I found out that when he was setting the fire at our church, he didn't personally plan to target our congregation. Since an active construction site lay in front of our building, he was drawn there to set the fire. It was just an opportunistic act, not a personal vendetta.

In any event, after I was informed that he had been arrested, I discovered his father had seen the composite drawing and put two and two together. Paul's father looked at his son's cell phone records and gas receipts and he realized that his son had been in many of the places where the fires had been. He went to the authorities and told them of his suspicions, and went with them to his son's apartment and asked his son to turn himself in, which he did. Thinking back, it must have been the most difficult thing any father would have to do in his entire life. Paul's father became overwhelmed with guilt and shame over his son doing this to the community and what the community had been through because of his son. He felt a real sense of failure as a parent.

There was eventually a movie produced, a CBS made-for-TV movie, about this whole story called "Not My Son." I had a chance to meet with the producers when they were in the area filming, but that's another story. The production featured the agony of the father having to make that decision and go through the process of getting his son arrested. I cover the topic in my book about both my frustrations and also the difficulties of how the media doesn't always tell the complete story, so people maybe got a skewed perspective of the process of healing and forgiveness we had been through.

When Paul was arrested, I felt drawn to visit him in jail while he was awaiting trial. I had often meditated on Jesus' Sermon on the Mount where he says, "Love your enemies." "You have heard that it was said, 'You shall love your neighbor and hate your enemy.' But I say to you, love your enemies and pray for those who persecute you ..." This kept rolling around in my mind, marinating in my heart. And I just felt drawn, compelled to visit Paul while he was in jail.

When I went to the county jail and they let me in to see him, Paul was stunned. He said, "Pastor, I can't believe you're here. Not after all the heartache I've caused you and your congregation." Then he said, "I've been sitting here in jail sober for the first time in months." Then everything just spilled out. He told me what he'd been going through and I could see everything from his perspective.

Paul told me he was going through a divorce, that his wife had run up his credit cards, and he knew he had to declare bankruptcy. He said that at 24, it felt like his life was just over. Then he shared with me how he had been sexually abused by a firefighter as a child. With all of the drinking he'd been doing, the stress, the depression, the self-hatred, the never-ending memories of abuse ... well, I think he just snapped. All this rage, self-loathing and anger had been building up in him.

He said, "I've been sitting here thinking about what I have done and I just, I felt, I've been reading my Bible and ... Pastor, do you think God can ever forgive me? Because I don't think

I can ever forgive myself."

I said, "Paul, you are a baptized child of God. God looks at you and sees only the cross of Jesus. God loves you. God still claims you."

With that, Paul broke down and he wept and he wept. Then he told me that he appreciated me being there for him and that my words meant more than I ever would realize. He said that he wanted to write a letter of apology to our congregation. I read his letter to the congregation the following Sunday. It set off in a chain of events—our leadership chose to write a letter of support directly to Paul and his family letting them all know that we were praying for Paul and that we were standing with him and his family during this difficult time.

The event of Paul's admission of his guilt and his seeking forgiveness began a whole new stage of the Spirit's work in our congregation from the grief work we still were doing, through the anger and the bargaining, to the point when we were ready to move forward. Our church found a new purpose and meaning for our existence, offering not only forgiveness for Paul, but establishing our ministry as a healing place for all those in the community.

Following Paul's arrest, we stood with him; I personally made a point to attend the sentencing hearings. In fact, I was called as a witness for both the prosecuting attorney and the defense attorney, which was interesting. As it happened, the judge let me do both at the same time—the prosecuting attorney got his statement, and then I was able to stay in the witness chair and the defense attorney got what he needed from me, not because I was there more for the defense, but because I was one of the victims too. In that way, I was able to testify to our pain and also serve as a witness for *Paul's pain.*

Some in our congregation and community asked whether I thought Paul was sincere in his apology. I know people who are manipulators, and Paul I'm sure would admit he's done his share of manipulation. But being as savvy I am at reading people, I never got any indication that he was simply playing us. I sensed that deep within him, he was both pained and remorseful, and I got the feeling that it was very genuine. Never did I excuse what Paul had done, either to our congregation or him personally, but knowing the abuse he went through, the pain he felt in his life, it placed his actions in context for me. I *understood.* Isn't that what learning to be a fellow human being is all about: understanding each other?

I think it also helped members of the congregation understand that Paul was a victim, as well. This realization is important because Paul's family had been ostracized from their own congregation, so we wanted to stand with them in solidarity to offer our support. Throughout the rebuilding process, we invited Paul's parents to be part of our rebuilding.

Now, forgiveness and healing, those two spiritual assets, they are a process. Learning to claim the assets as your own is not something that's just instantly done. In the first half of my book, I spell out the five stages of forgiveness to tell the story. Then in the second half, I continue the story, but I talk about the process I personally went through, and also what all of us did together because forgiveness, healing, reconciliation—all of these—are a process, a journey.

Paul was sentenced to life in prison, and I continued to visit him in his incarceration. I would see him usually about every other month. It started out by offering words of encouragement and to see how he was doing. Initially, of course, he was quite despondent, but then I encouraged him to get in touch with the prison chaplain, which he did. In addition to the visits, we were corresponding on a regular basis, which we've continued to do to this day.

Through our letters and visits, he began sharing how the impact of our congregation's forgiveness completely transformed his outlook on his life. He recognized that God did love him, and in an even more tangible way that God's love had come to him *through us*. Realizing this began to transform his entire perception about his purpose. He took courses on theology through the prison chaplain's office, and then he started leading Bible studies and helping with worship. Music has always been one of his great joys and strengths, so today he directs the prison choir and plays the piano for worship every Sunday. He's shared with me that he can spot the difference between people who are just using the prison chaplain or the worship for their own means, and those who are genuinely hurting and looking for healing and reconciliation in their lives.

After I had been visiting him for a while and sharing about the book that I was writing and getting his input—I wanted him to be very much aware of what I was writing, and so involving him in that whole process as I was able— just before my book was published, my wife died of ovarian cancer. I had written Paul and shared this fact with him. I visited him probably a month or so after her memorial service. For three hours or so as we visited, while I was still in the throes of grief, I realized that Paul was ministering to me.

The power of somebody who had been transformed by the love of God and Christ's forgiveness had taken the role of ministering to the minister. Truthfully, he became *my pastor* in that time. He counseled me, we read scripture together, prayed with me, and simply was present to encourage and support me through this new loss. Paul had become the wounded Body of Christ—God's love, incarnate—when I needed it most.

Of course, once again, I spent some time railing at God after my wife died as well, saying, "You know … first you burn down my church and then you take the love of my life away from me!" But, I took great solace from the Psalms, knowing that

David, too, railed against God. I kept reminding God: "I'm not Job. I don't want to be your new Job!" And interestingly enough, I had just finished spiritual direction at a Benedictine center north of Olympia, Washington. There, too, being part of a group I was able to share my pain of both going through my wife's illness and then her death.

Today I've remarried and have continued to serve as a pastor. One great joy and privilege has been to be able to share this story across the country at various congregations. In one situation, an ELCA congregation just outside of Madison, Wisconsin lost their church to an arsonist. The young pastor and his wife were graduates of Wartburg Seminary and somehow knew about our story. They invited me to come out to meet with the congregation. I preached on our story of healing and forgiveness and meet with their leadership team. We also talked about some practical considerations how to help the congregation to move forward. I've also lead various retreats and seminars on the healing power of forgiveness.

I've shared this all with Paul and, in fact, most recently I was in Everett, Washington, where Paul's originally from and where his father had his business. The congregation there invited me to come and preach about our story. People were just blown away. People said, "I knew Paul's dad." Some people knew Paul when he was a young kid and had never heard the rest of the story: that it didn't just end with the fire and Paul in prison, but that Paul's life had been transformed and that others' lives were being transformed because of this story.

Forgiveness continues to add to the story, to create a resurrection life out of something horrible. Thinking back on it all, the events have transformed not only in my ministry, my role as a pastor; they've become the most defining moments of my life.

When I began research for this book, I looked to multiple resources for information about forgiveness. That was the easy part; whole mountains of books have been written on the topic from nearly every angle you can imagine. The hard part was finding a candidate to interview. Although most people have some story of forgiveness, I wanted the one I included in this book to show how forgiveness as a spiritual asset lends itself to the concept of resilience.

As Rick shared his story, new questions began to pop up. What difficulties did Rick encounter in his decision to forgive Paul? How had forgiveness defined not just his ministry, but influenced his life positively? Why is forgiveness so hard to do when it feels so *good* to hold onto resentments? And of course, I wanted to know how forgiveness as a spiritual asset undergirded Rick's ability to bounce back after further trauma, such as when his wife died from ovarian cancer.

The first question I pose above—whether there were difficulties that arose—Rick answered simply by sharing the ongoing story.

"I want to mention that I just saw Paul last week. A reunion after 11 years and he was just so grateful. We spent probably six, seven hours together. I hadn't seen him face to face because I was in Arizona and we just moved back to the Seattle area this past December.

"We continued to correspond over that time, but we hadn't seen each other specifically. And so it was a reunion of sorts; he was just so gracious and gave me so many giant bear hugs. We had just a wonderful conversation and you know, kind of caught up on each other's lives. He shared again how much my support, prayers, forgiveness, and letters of encouragement have meant to him over the years. But then he shared some pain and struggle he's experienced over his family, that he's not seen his parents for well over a year now."

I asked, "What happened with his parents?"

He said, "They have seen him off and on, but it's the difficulties his father has gone through. He ended up probably losing his business and destroying his reputation. It was the stigma of Paul, who was the main customer point-of-contact. All the big clients just chose to walk away. When they used up most of their savings and mortgaged their home to pay for Paul's attorneys during the hearing process; they went through their own trauma of dealing with their son's crime and the shame that they felt. It was all very public and his mother was in counseling for a long time.

"Beyond that, the news media still tends to haunt them. There was a television company that contacted them and wanted to do a follow-up piece now, almost 25 years later, and Paul cautioned them about it because knows the tendency of the media to want to sensationalize things."

Rick made this point of the media's intentional manipulation several times during our interview. He would know; he's taken part in many productions from BBC to Oprah.

He continued, "And the television producers this time around presented it to the parents as a chance to tell their side of the story and set the record straight. But when it came out sometime this past winter, they just focused on the drama with Paul. I think the title of the episode was 'Evil Lives Within.' The whole thing again opened up the wounds that his parents have had over all of this."

"So how did that affect Paul's relationship with his parents?" I asked. I could see that forgiveness and healing with the family is not only more complex but painful.

Rick said, "Oh yes. Like I said, it's been a year-plus since he's seen them and Paul thinks he's to blame for his parents' pain and difficulties. You know, he's trying to reconcile with his parents and saying, 'I'm sorry I'm sorry, I'm sorry.' But I just keep telling him, 'Paul, it's not you. It's the fact that your father blames himself and cannot forgive himself.' A person has got to get to the point where they're able to forgive themselves because they have already been forgiven. Paul's father doesn't recognize that he's been forgiven for being a failure as a parent."

Rick told me how it was a whole new insight for Paul to recognize the pain his father was feeling wasn't necessarily just because of what Paul had done, but that every person needs to go through the process of learning to forgive themselves, too.

I then asked Rick how—since Paul's father hasn't yet worked through learning to forgive himself—that it has made Paul's father *less* resilient or continued to cause heartache and stress in his life.

"Absolutely, absolutely. For whatever reason, he hasn't gotten to that place yet. He needs to, eventually. Because, at least according to Paul, the guilt is destroying him. And it's not anything necessarily that Paul, I, or anyone can do about it. Each person needs to come to this recognition on their own. We can help facilitate it. We can educate. We can pray. But a person has got to recognize and claim it for themselves."

I asked, "So let me get to the point then: how does the spiritual asset of forgiveness influence or affect a person's—or even a community's—ability to bounce back after stress and trauma?"

Over the phone, I heard Rick sigh. I hated to put him on the spot, but this question was the main one I'm asking in this book. Rick is a highly-educated, well-read and spiritually-focused guy. I suppose it shouldn't have surprised me that he'd answer by citing something he's read.

"Well, there's been a lot written on resilience. In terms of what the literature says, some people seem more prone to being more resilient as part of their DNA, and other people maybe not so much. I mean, we all have the capacity, but some just seem to fit into it better than others. So ... I think part of it is who we are by nature as an individual. But then there's another piece of it, the spiritual factor, that God offers the gift of resilience. We can allow the Spirit to work in our lives to receive that gift or we can reject that gift."

One of the things that I have discovered in my research for this book is that any human being has an innate power within them to be resilient to many awful changes. How people embrace it, though—how each brain is wired—differs among people. Rick's statement that everyone has the potential to be resilient is true. What that looks like with each person though depends on many things. Where Paul accepted Rick's and the congregation's forgiveness for him, Paul's father still was processing his forgiveness for himself. In fact, Rick had more to say about all this.

"There's a second piece of resilience, the spiritual factor that I mentioned, where God offers us through God's Spirit, the gift of reconciliation. We can grab onto it to help us move forward … or not. I mention in my book a little bit about how some people get stuck in the victim stage, which is where I think Paul's dad has been. The book *Great Expectations* deals with this whole thing with the character Miss Havisham who becomes crystallized in the past's disappointments and sorrows. She's never able to move on, but is just stuck."

It led me to think how *that* topic would make a great sequel to this book—how spiritual obstacles or blocks can hinder our development to be an authentic human being. Brushing any overly-optimistic aspirations off, I asked Rick point-blank: "How did forgiveness for you, personally, help you in the initial stages after you knew it was an arsonist who burned down your church?"

"I guess my personal spirituality, my piety, that God is not a God that doesn't care about what happens, but that God does care about us as individuals. You know, sometimes I'll rail at God saying, 'What the heck are you thinking?!' or, 'Where have you been? We needed you!' I think it's important to acknowledge that feeling, the sense of abandonment and desolation."

Rick also said that forgiveness was a spiritual process, and not something he instantly recognized.

"And I've journaled. Oh my gosh, I journaled those questions after the fire and after the loss of my wife. By journaling, I could theologically reflect on what was happening in my spirit as well as turning to scripture and being part of a support group." You have to be proactive in terms of going through that journey and knowing that it was, indeed, a journey and a process and that I would somehow come out on the other side. But, yes, I had to do the work. Congregations have to do the work, too, you know."

I asked him to say more.

"Well, yes. Several times we had subsequent services of healing and forgiveness when we invited Paul's father and mother to come together with some of the victims of our church's fire. Then Paul's father was awarded a $25,000 reward, which was the Arson Task Force reward for turning in his son. And, of course, he didn't want to accept it— that was blood money for him. So he gave a portion of the reward to our congregation because we had been so supportive of his family and Paul.

"I think the actions of our congregation holding an opportunity to walk on this journey together with Paul's family, and his father being able to gift the money … it was a way for him to express his regret and his apologies to the community. We held this as a service, too. I called up the various leaders in the congregation and he handed them the check. It was a powerful symbol. I mean we orchestrated that, it wasn't his idea. But the ritual of presenting the check offered a sense of meaning, not just for him, but for us too. Forgiveness is a process of rebuilding of people's lives to learn to live in reconciliation with each other, despite what happened. Honestly, if we hadn't done the work—traveled on this journey—we couldn't have moved forward."

The discussion then led to some of the other questions I still had. I asked Rick, "What if Paul had not been receptive to you coming? Would it have been different? Would you still have forgiven him?"

"Those are good questions. I don't know, I really don't. It certainly made it a lot easier knowing that he was remorseful. And it made it easier for me to be kind of a public witness to the healing power of forgiveness and its ability to make me a more whole, resilient person. Resentment, hatred, not forgiving … they can be really destructive, obviously. But, as I said, the journey of forgiveness was a defining moment of my ministry and has been the defining moment of who I am. It reaffirmed that I am a person of healing and reconciliation and that is what our Creator intends for all of us."

Resilience and Forgiveness

When former President Bill Clinton had asked Nelson Mandela, the South African anti-apartheid revolutionary, how he was able to forgive his captors, Mandela replied, "When I walked out of the gate I knew that if I continued to hate these people I was still in prison."[30] More than anything, if you decide not to forgive, the potential is set to create a prison of your own resentment and anger. In Rick's case, he stated that he was compelled to act. He simply *had* to meet with Paul after he discovered the truth about the tragedy of losing the church building to a cruel act of arson.

One point I kept challenging Rick with in the interview was that it all seemed too easy to me for Rick to forgive Paul after what he had done. Sure, I was getting the whole of the story, something that took place over a period of years, not

---

[30] Remnick, David . "Bill Clinton's Quest to Save the World, Reclaim His Legacy—and Elect His Wife." *The New Yorker*, September 18, 2006.

experiencing it as it happened as he had; I know that it was a long process for him too. However, as one person who as easily holds resentments as I do (I sometimes stay pissed when I take my kid to school and the traffic is bad) the challenge I met was fully understanding how the process of letting go of the hurt turned into *real* forgiveness. What I discovered—both in hearing Rick's story and through the reading I've done on this topic—is forgiveness isn't a feeling, it's a deliberate act of faith and a choice.

At least how a reader experiences him in the Gospels, Jesus of Nazareth was pretty big on forgiveness. Take this account from the Gospel of Luke:

Be on your guard! If another disciple sins, you must rebuke the offender, and if there is repentance, you must forgive. And if the same person sins against you seven times a day, and turns back to you seven times and says, 'I repent,' you must forgive.[31]

The Gospel account in Matthew is even bigger on forgiveness: "Jesus said to [Peter], 'Not seven times, but, I tell you, seventy-seven times.'"[32]

The apostles' response in Luke is what really interests me here though. In the story, they respond with utter shock at such a ridiculous command. "Increase our faith!"[33] They seem to cry out in hopeless despair that they cannot forgive a person who makes the same mistake over and over, but continues to genuinely seek absolution. As a person in recovery, I can relate. My wife, Carol, in my estimation is a saint for all the times she forgave my antics, lying, and general malfeasance in the drama that is addiction. Where the line is drawn between forgiveness and co-dependence is beyond the scope of this chapter. Still, I understand the apostles' surprise and call for Jesus to wave a

---

[31] Luke 17:3, 4 NRSV
[32] Matt. 18:22 NRSV
[33] Luke 17:5 NRSV

magic wand to increase their capacity to forgive. Their plea to increase their faith is spot on though—forgiveness isn't instantly feeling all nice and chummy again with the person who has harmed us; it's a journey of reconciliation and it takes work. Hard work.

If I learned nothing else from Rick's story, I discovered that he was just as apprehensive going into that jail cell the first time to visit Paul. His decision to visit Paul was an act of faith. Things could have turned sour, but Rick acted because, as a follower of Jesus, he could do nothing else. As it turned out (although unusually quickly, I'd add), Paul was not only receptive to Rick's visit but also responded positively to Rick's forgiveness for the heinous acts he had done. But that didn't mean the work for both parties was over. Not at all.

The healing for the community needed more time and effort from everyone. That's reconciliation. Reconciliation and healing need to follow the act of forgiveness. And reconciliation and healing aren't necessarily tied to emotions, either. The pattern that I see is that through the hard work of forgiveness and reconciliation, the freedom of healing eventually follows.

The Christian tradition doesn't hold proprietary rights on forgiveness, of course. In the beginning of this chapter, I lift up the Buddhist tradition of letting go of dangerous and caustic resentments and anger. Similarly, Islam holds the belief that God is "... most merciful and oft forgiving."[34] In fact, most religions highlight that forgiveness is not just "important," but a central part of what it means to live as an authentic human being. Even rationalism embraces the idea that to live without forgiveness for others ultimately only hurts yourself. It's clear that, whatever your beliefs, forgiveness is a good thing and probably a healthy attitude to have in life. The question remains: how does forgiveness become a spiritual asset to undergird a

---

[34] Qur'an 49:15

person's resilience?

In Rick's case, forgiveness and reconciliation were central to his ability to bounce back after further trauma or stress. He made this point most clear to me in relating how Paul had become a force of healing for him after he had lost his wife to ovarian cancer. Before you read over too quickly, I want you to reflect on what really happened and what that means—a serial arsonist who had burned down a church, a place of worship, and one who had a history of abuse and manipulation, became God's healing presence for a person he had victimized.

The event is nothing short of miraculous, and in fact, *is* a miracle. The Greek word for *miracle* in the New Testament is *semeion*, which means *sign*. Paul's transformation into a force of healing and good for Rick in his time of need is a sign of something greater in play, which we do not necessarily understand. For me, as a believer, it points to the work of something greater than myself, God.

When I asked Rick whether he thought he would have been able to come through the loss of his wife in the same way without Paul's ministering to him, his answer was an unequivocal no. Paul's presence was just as necessary for him to move forward with his life as working with a professional therapy group.

However, I need to add that forgiveness, for many, doesn't seem as tidy and clear as it does in Rick's story. (Although, as I mentioned, it took many years and a load of work for him, too.) When I think of Cathy's story, the first chapter of this book, I imagine that forgiveness for her attacker would be perhaps more difficult. I followed up with Cathy on this point. Since beginning to write this book, a lot has happened. For one, she faced her attacker at the trial and still has yet to write a victim-impact statement. Also, her attacker has been sentenced to one term of life in prison for the assault and most probably faces a second life-term for the kidnapping charge in the State of Mississippi.

Cathy shared that, yes, she did forgive him for what he had done. However, she also told me that the act wasn't easy. "I cried and cried," she said. She also said that in her church she admitted having difficulty moving on after the incident. In an altar-call type situation, she stated that she once and for all forgave him. Not that I in any way doubt her sincerity, it just strikes me that her journey for forgiveness still has miles left on its path. My hope for her now, as she seeks to use her story to reach out to women in similar situations, she'll one day be able to completely heal the spiritual trauma she's had to endure. I don't envy her, but I'm certainly inspired by her willingness to help others.

In the case of violent trauma, there have been studies done to show that forgiveness is positively correlated with the ability to thrive, and has a negative correlation with adverse PTSD symptoms. The difficulty, as always, is quantifying the results to show how much or in what manner a spiritual asset, such as forgiveness, aids resilience. They only show that forgiveness and the process of reconciliation do indeed make a difference with a person's resilience, not "how much."[35]

So, what's the takeaway from all of this? The primary reason for writing this book has been to show the stories how spiritual assets, such as forgiveness, have the ability to allow us to see more clearly, love more deeply, and act more courageously. These stories highlight how spiritual assets make us more resilient to the trauma and difficult experiences life inevitably throws at us. No doubt, both of these assertions have been fulfilled for Rick. He is a healthier and more resilient person not simply by what happened to him and having gotten through it, but instead also by his proactive response—he made a decision

---

[35] Connor, Kathryn M., Jonathan R.T. Davidson, and Li-Ching Lee. 2003. "Spirituality, Resilience, and Anger in Survivors of Violent Trauma: A Community Survey." *Journal of Traumatic Stress* 16 (5): 487-94.

to forgive Paul because to do otherwise was contrary to his beliefs. And because of that forgiveness, Rick also benefited in becoming a more resilient person after the death of his wife.

How can forgiveness provide a resilience-building presence in each of our lives? I think much of that has to do with our understanding that we don't have to "feel good" about taking the action, at least initially. In my own experience, I've had to make amends for idiotic, impulsive actions. I'm not just talking about the actions I did while I was spiraling out of control in my addiction, either. Living a sober lifestyle has meant for me that I no longer get to act like a jackass and simply brush it off. And let me tell you, I can still act like a jerk with the best of them.

One instance comes to mind is how I tend to behave with anything customer service related. It must have happened about four years ago. I had to call our credit card company to fix an error I had found in our statement. I'd been on hold for about twenty minutes and was already steaming for the time I'd spent in dealing with the issue. What set me off was the customer-service reps insistence that it wasn't the company's error. Like a switch thrown in my brain, I got high off of getting indignant (and, in reality, this is exactly what's happening inside my brain as it is flooded with dopamine). After a dopamine-fueled rant, I slammed the phone on the floor in self-righteous indigence.

After three or four minutes of cooling off, the guilt hit. Since I already had the customer service representative's employee number, I called back, waited on hold—again—and, after speaking with a supervisor, stated that I wanted to apologize for my bad behavior. It didn't "feel good" to make the call. In fact, it was difficult! Surprisingly, I got in contact with the person and apologized profusely for my poor behavior.

Now, this took place on the opposite side of forgiveness. Like Paul with Rick, I took the time to communicate that I was sorry for how I had acted. However, as a person who wants to act in accordance with his own spiritual asset of honesty, I had to get honest with myself and admit that I acted like a jerk. The customer service rep forgave me and I was able to move on from the incident. The joy of forgiveness is when both sides can benefit from the action. The benefits I garnered were that I didn't have to let the resentment eat at me, and I received the gift of being forgiven by the other person.

Oh yeah, as it turned out, I was wrong assuming that the company was at fault. I had misread the credit card statement.

Resilience to life's difficulties, stresses, and in some cases traumas, comes through the spiritual actions we take to offer a new view, a new perspective. Forgiveness grants us that new perspective because it allows us to free ourselves from the bondage of a closely held resentment or anger will inevitably place us in. Resilience is also learning to be flexible to the mistakes that others make, even when those mistakes may harm us irreparably. Forgiveness is the willingness to move on, to let the past be the past, not because we don't care about justice, but because without forgiveness and healing, those past harms can continue to harm us.

Chapter Six

Love

One experience in 2005 I rarely reveal to people outside Twelve Step meetings. I was heavily abusing painkillers at the time. One evening, I took more pills than usual and I fell asleep. Suddenly, I woke up gasping for air. The way I felt is difficult to describe—it was almost as if reality took on a surreal quality. My throat and skull felt like they were being crushed. I had an impending sense of doom. My heart raced in panic and didn't stop for at least ten minutes after I sat up, shaking. Looking back, the feeling mimicked death. I'd felt what it would be like to die, completely alone.

Neurologists have named the subjective experience I believe I encountered *derealization*, a dissociative disorder with multiple causes. One of these is *hypoxia*, or lack of oxygen to the brain. The opioid-based drugs flowing through my blood affected my body's ability to regulate breathing. That night, I probably overdosed and came very close to ceasing to breathe at all. Today, I believe I nearly died. If I had taken one more pill, I very well may have.

Since getting sober, I sometimes think about that terrifying experience. I've wondered how I would have hurt my family and my friends had I died. On more than one occasion, I have personally lost men whom I've sponsored in AA and NA to overdoses and accidents. I witnessed firsthand the effect their deaths had on their loved ones. I think that's part of addiction: drug addicts or alcoholics don't realize how traumatic their deaths will be for people who love them. The exploration of the trauma of losing a person you love to drug addiction strikes me as a fitting topic for the final chapter of this book. I started this book's introduction with my story, which ended far differently.

I met Jennifer Maurer (our shared last name is purely coincidental) in an online support group for people affected by addiction. The group has given me new insight into the urgency of the problem we're facing as a country. Over 100 people die of drug overdoses every day in the United States. That figure doesn't take into consideration the deaths from alcohol abuse from accidents or alcohol poisoning, either. When you add those deaths in, it comes to nearly 15 deaths every hour of every day that a person dies as a direct result of addiction.[36]

Statistics don't mean much on paper; they're just abstract numbers. However, when someone you love becomes a statistic, the numbers make you realize you're not alone in your loss. Jennifer shared her story with me in the hope that her son Michael's death might move others to understand the urgency of the problem, and also because of how much she loved him. She hoped you would empathize with her love for her son and the profound pain of losing him to addiction. For Jennifer, love was the spiritual asset through which she discovered healing, purpose, meaning, and resilience.

I interviewed Jennifer via phone on several occasions from her home in Richmond, Indiana. Her gentle voice revealed a deep spirituality grounded in her Catholic upbringing. She's a teacher by vocation, but only recently returned to work after having lost Michael on September 11, 2016. His death is still very raw; she mentioned that she often cries when she wakes

---

[36] Source: *NIH – National Institute on Drug Abuse.* Retrieved on Jan. 15, 2017.

in the morning, realizing once again that her only son is gone. However, I discerned through our conversations that she is just beginning to discover how her love for Michael might become her greatest strength. She's learning that she can help herself and others who have experienced loss. She turns her love outward, and it opens a new world for her.

Jennifer's Story

Next to a tree, in the middle of an abandoned lot, in the worst neighborhood in Miami, I lost my son. Sometimes I close my eyes and I can imagine the place. I've even observed the exact spot from my phone on a satellite map. I can see every moment in my mind as it must have played out. First, Michael approaches a homeless man, asking him for drugs. The man declines. Then the homeless man watches Michael make contact with someone else: someone who sells him the drugs. I see my son smoking from a glass pipe. He begins to act strangely. Then, he's rolling and convulsing on the ground. The homeless man tries to shake him into awareness. But Michael just lies there, unmoving.

I see the rescue team arriving minutes later, but unable to bring him back.

Him. Always him.

In the middle of a hot day on September 11, 2016, my son, Michael, died of a drug overdose. He had gone to Fort Lauderdale to enter rehab for probably the eighth time in the past several years. This time it was at a place called Faith Farm. He arrived at the campus on Friday, September 2. Since it was a holiday weekend, they were unable to complete his intake until September 6. He called me that day, in fact.

When I saw the number from Faith Farm pop up on my

caller ID, I was at work and immediately worried that they were calling to give me bad news. *Had he already left?* I honestly did not expect to hear from him for 30 days, since that was the rehabilitation center's policy. He reassured me that he had arrived safely, and was getting admitted. That was the last time I heard my son's voice.

Almost two weeks later, I received the letter I had mailed to him on the 10th. It was marked *Return-to-Sender – No Longer Resides Here.* I remember staring at that letter, tears making their way down my cheeks. I went inside my house and called Faith Farm immediately. They informed me that he had left the facility on September 9. Michael had only made it one full week. *What happened? Was he safe?*

The next evening, a phone call came in from Miami-Dade County. I assumed it was the county jail. In a way, I was relieved, because at least I would know where Michael was and that he was safe. Instead of the jail, it was the medical examiner's office.

After asking a few questions to verify that I was Michael's mother, a kind woman said the words no parent should ever have to hear: "Mrs. Maurer, I regret to inform you that your son, Michael, passed away here in Miami, on September 11." There was an immediate shift in my consciousness—at that moment, even as I wailed, I knew that my entire life had changed.

Michael didn't have an ideal childhood, but he had a good one. There were scratches and some sizable dents: two divorces and hurt feelings left the most bruises. Regardless, Michael came from the best kind of people on both sides of his family— loving, responsible people who put each other first. By the time Michael turned 15, we were working hard to navigate some terrifying waters. The storm of addiction was already coming.

Michael's story of addiction is similar to many others. From the time he was introduced to marijuana, he was initiated into a whole new existence that I was completely unprepared for as his mother. I have never even smoked cigarettes, much less been a recreational drug user. Michael often told me that once he had a taste of weed, there was no turning back. He liked it too much. He liked the way it made him feel.

Similar to others who suffer from the disease of addiction, it didn't take long for Michael's initial choice to use drugs and alcohol to become a compulsion. Next came drinking. Then all types of pills. Then cocaine. Something you need to know about Michael is that he had always been a stubborn child. He'd always been challenging for me, but I loved him. When Michael was four, my father even bought me a book called *Parenting the Strong Willed Child*. Michael did not give up on anything. If he wanted something, he pursued it until he got it. I believe that this stubbornness affected his drug use, too.

Ever since he died, many of his friends have told me that he was completely fearless. He had no fear of anything because he was going to be the big guy on the block. He liked to show off, but it was more than that—of his friends; he was the first to take whatever drug he could find, and he would take the most. I don't believe this behavior was something he set out to do intentionally. What I mean is that the drugs turned him into a different person—one who lived dangerously.

People told me he would do anything. Someone could come up to him with a handful of pills and say, "You gotta try this," and he'd just take it all, not even knowing what it was. It was very risky behavior. Michael just liked being high.

The other important aspect behind Michael's drug use was his mental health diagnoses. He suffered from OCD and possibly ADD. I believe that it's conceivable that he was self-medicating to alleviate the stress these illnesses caused him. His obsessive-compulsive side I think also contributed to his drug use.

He became obsessed with it—first with marijuana, then with other drugs. He wanted to do it all day every day. It wasn't a weekend party, pass-the-joint-around kind of thing. He'd leave school in the middle of class to smoke weed. He began getting in trouble, not going to school, and skipping class. At one point, my parents took him in for a short time, but even they had to give him up.

Michael dropped out at the beginning of junior year. He had so few credits he couldn't even be considered a freshman. His intelligence served him well, though, and he decided during one of his many incarcerations to take the GED without studying. He passed with high marks. Michael spent long hours, days, and weeks either in juvenile detention, or juvenile court. His feelings also continually flipped. He either hated me and made my life hell, or he'd act like the most loving, generous, compassionate son a mother can imagine.

We gave him several cars, which eventually all had to be sold. We only wanted to help him, but he just couldn't seem to stay clean and sober. By the time he was 17, he had been in so much trouble that one judge was determined to send him to a prison for boys. I wrote the judge a letter, begging him to send Michael somewhere for help for his addiction. Much to my surprise, the judge responded to my plea by allowing Michael to spend the following nine months at a treatment center in Wabash, Indiana. There, he was housed with other juvenile drug addicts and seemed to be doing well.

Because the treatment center was for juveniles, Michael had to be released when he turned 18. Within two weeks of his release, he was arrested on four separate charges and headed to jail—only this time, he was tried as an adult. When he was 19, he got high and attempted to rob a Burger King. For that crime, he was sentenced to 18 months in prison, but he only had to complete nine. After that, he moved with his girlfriend to Dayton, Ohio. His step-father and I helped the two get an apartment together and Michael got a job. He seemed very happy and settled. However, the relief for me that he was finally getting his life together was short-lived.

At some point during that year, Michael found heroin. Maybe it was the other way around: heroin found him. By that time, Michael had done most kinds of drugs, but not heroin. Someone told me that he was initially reluctant to stick a needle into his arm, but wanted to try it. What happened in that moment would alter Michael's life—all our lives—in unimaginable ways. He spiraled into an addiction so consuming, it destroyed everything in its path.

A few months after he began using this drug, he came home to borrow my car for a court appointment. I was utterly shocked at his appearance—his body was emaciated and his skin reflected a sickly, gray color. He was also sweating profusely and his eyes were dilated. He couldn't stand still and talked as if he would never stop, rambling. He also never stopped scratching his skin. Never, in all the years we had been dealing with his addiction, had I seen him in such bad shape. It terrified me. This was the beginning of years of terror and tears and estrangement. A few months later, I resigned from my teaching position after eight years. It was impossible for me to focus on anything but Michael's illness and his struggle.

Heroin broke my son into a thousand pieces; there was no repairing him. No matter what we tried—repeated trips to rehab programs, halfway houses, giving him jobs and places to live and vehicles to use, medications, Suboxone or methadone maintenance—nothing worked. Nothing. His addiction imprisoned him in a cell with no walls, one that was so tightly sealed that he could never get out.

He had used so much over the past four years before his

death that his brain was depleted of the dopamine necessary to help him feel good or happy about anything. I have learned this is why heroin is so deadly and all consuming. The addiction takes hold quickly, and because it takes the brain time to make more dopamine, the withdrawals are terrible. When a heroin user is without it for a couple of days, they go through the wringer—achy bones and joints, horrible nausea, diarrhea, sweating, and itching are common symptoms. Using even a small amount made Michael feel much better; so it became a cycle. A deadly one. Heroin led to meth and crack. He even became homeless and wandered the streets. He was treading along the shadows, and as his addiction got darker, I became more desperate.

I couldn't save my son. No matter how much I loved him or what I tried—so many times and in so many ways—I never seemed to learn my lesson. After trying to give it to God, I still found myself trying to control the situation by not allowing him to go hungry or wear dirty clothes. Somehow, even though he wasn't living with me and he was no longer welcome to do so, I still had trouble drawing the "line in the sand." I suppose all parents struggling with a child who is addicted discover how far they can or won't go. I remember multiple times clearly explaining to anyone who would listen that there were certain things I couldn't bring myself to do, and letting my son go hungry was one of them.

I would discover that Michael had been hungry many times because in all the places he lived, the one place where he felt at ease, accepted, and could stay sober—in Florida—ended up being the place that sent him to the streets and eventually took his life.

Faith Farm is a Florida-based, Christian program for men struggling with addiction. Michael thought the world of the program and seemed to be doing well; in fact, it was the longest he ever made it in a program of any kind—five months.

Eventually, his disease got the better of him. I don't know what happened, but he must have just felt compelled to use again.

When he left Faith Farm, things really took a turn for the worse. It became a nightmare of homelessness because he wouldn't stay in one place and if he was on the street, he was seeking drugs again. I've since learned that Michael did things he was ashamed of to survive, like steal money from a dead body on the street. Other things too, which haunted him. Florida was a bad place for him.

It was bad for me, too, because I didn't know where he was or whether he was even alive or not. I prayed for him. I prayed so hard! I wanted God to know that my son needed watching over, that he wasn't going hungry, and I prayed that *somehow* everything would work out for the better. Every time my prayers seemed to be answered, Michael would end up going back to drugs, and that just crushed us. But, it also crushed him. After a while, Michael knew he was an addict—a bad one—and he hated who he was.

My mother and I flew to Miami to bring him home after we found out that Michael had cancer. He was diagnosed during a brief stint in a hospital detox facility. What mother in her right mind would be overjoyed to discover her son had cancer? Well, I was! Because I thought the diagnosis was the wake-up call he desperately needed. I imagined that he would finally choose his life over his addiction. It made me happy to finally be able to take care of my son.

But within two weeks of being home, after getting insurance and a good doctor and a round of chemo, Michael began to use heroin again. And, once again, I had to ask my son to leave my home, because I knew what would happen if he stayed. Drugs took him away from us even while he was alive. Drugs made him unpredictable and unstable and untrustworthy. Drugs stole his identity—even though he was our son, we felt like we were confronting a stranger.

Anyone who loves an addict will recognize the reality of the horror of addiction: someone you love is no longer that person. Michael's behavior was becoming more erratic and he was staying up all night—not sleeping for days, not eating, and of course using. I always knew. The drug affected him very differently than it does most people. He didn't do the nodding out thing. It made him hyper, made him feel like he was on top of the world. It stimulated him and turned him into someone else.

I believe that, in his heart, Michael was—and always had been—a good person. He was genuine. He was caring. He had such empathy and compassion. I could tell he felt remorse for the things he had done and he constantly revealed to me that he was sorry. He never wanted to be the person he turned into when he used. He often said, "Do you think I want to be this person? I hate who I am, and I hate what I've done to my life, and I hate what I'm doing to you and to the rest of the family!" I saw glimmers of hope that he could change, that one day he would go on and help others with their problems. Although he would always find a place to go get help, he never could stick it out. He just couldn't do it. I spent so much time the last 13 years asking *why* and wondering what else could have been done to help him.

After the summer of his cancer diagnosis, Michael went to jail in November. This time, it was in our hometown, for theft. I had begged him to do something to get off the street. He spent six months in jail, and during that time, we exchanged dozens of letters and had many talks and visits. We always had a strong, close relationship when he was forced into sobriety. When he was locked up, my real son had once again reemerged.

When he got out, he went straight into a non-profit program in Richmond called Hope House. He was able to join us on weekends for home visits, and we decided that as long as he was there and stayed clean and sober, he was welcome. He was able to spend about five weekends with us during that time. I was overjoyed by his presence.

On Father's Day in 2016, he met up with a friend and came to the cookout high on drugs. It only took one minute for me to determine what was going on. He confessed his transgression and didn't get kicked out of Hope House, but we told him he could not have home visits anymore. By the Fourth of July weekend, he left Hope House, moved in with a friend, and began using heavily again. I have found myself feeling thankful to God that seven out of the last nine months of his life were happy ones with him. I could not have said that the years before then.

Everything came to a head in late August—Michael and I had a conversation about how he was feeling that was so disturbing and so frightening, I sought out a therapist for an official intervention. He told me about all the shame he carried, and he cried, telling me he had done such terrible things. All I could do was give him another chance, hoping beyond hope that something would change. The intervention took place the last week of August, with my family present, and Michael agreed to get the necessary help while the family agreed (at the therapist's prompting) to step away until he got better. I took him to the bus station in Dayton, hugged him and told him I loved him, shed a few tears, and breathed a sigh of relief as I drove home.

I'll never forget what I emphatically stated to my husband the night before he left: "I have to be the one to take him to that bus. Don't you understand? It could very well be the last time I ever see my son again."

And it was.

My conversation with Michael prior to the intervention helped me to understand that there were demons he was battling that went beyond his addiction. This lent a sense of urgency to the situation for me. I can remember holding his tear-stained face and saying, "Don't you understand, Michael, that there is nothing, *nothing* you could ever do that God wouldn't forgive? And don't you understand that there is nothing you could ever do that would make me think less of you or feel less love for you? I am your mother—I'll always love you. Can't you try to accept that and forgive yourself?"

As angry as I was that day—he had gone to the clinic for his dose of methadone *and* shot up heroin and was worse than I had ever seen him—I needed him to know that I would always love him and that God forgives anyone for anything. It nearly destroyed me to see his anguish that day. Although Michael knew God, he had trouble accepting that he was deserving of God's forgiveness, mercy, and grace. I have to believe that he realizes that now, in heaven.

When I think about my son now, I don't see an addict. I see a young man who was in a lot of pain and who hated his life. I see a man who suffered an illness, but who felt both weak and prideful. I see a man who was in constant turmoil and who often felt alone. I see a guilty man who carried a burden of shame and anguish that destroyed him as much as the drugs ever did.

As his mother, my heart aches deeply for not always being able to see that man when he was still alive. I knew he was hurting. It was a very hard place to be—always in the middle, between my son who I desperately wanted to care for, and everyone around me telling me to cut ties, including the many recovering addicts I had shared his story with over the years. But I was his mother: *I knew Michael.* I knew that cutting ties would never make a difference.

I spend a lot of time today playing the wishing game. For example, I wish I wouldn't have felt so resentful of having to bring him food. All my resentment seemed to accomplish was to put him on the defensive and make him feel like less of a person than he already felt about himself. What was the point of my negativity back then? I have learned that once we have decided to give, all of our emotion should be in the giving itself. We can't freely give something and then resent doing it, because then it becomes about us. Giving should always be about the receiver, period, and should be done with love. While I know in my heart that Michael knew my love for him and felt my compassion, today I wonder what would have happened if I hadn't shown a hint of resentment. Would it have made a difference?

The struggle over Michael's death has shown me what it means to truly be sorry for something. I have always been the type of person who is willing and able to admit when I am wrong and to apologize for that wrong; however, true contrition is *felt*, not declared. Because the situation warrants it, I have done a serious accounting of my life with my son, and I have found some areas to be lacking. For any failure on my part as his mother, I have learned true contrition. To be truly sorrowful is as painful as it is cleansing. I don't really have the words to describe it, just the certainty that I am feeling it deep in my soul. It is part of my grief. I have to find a way to face it and to know that *God* forgives me and that *Michael* forgives me as well.

Almost daily, I can picture his face, and I see his heart and how broken he was. I feel his sense of anguish. Michael must have been crying out to God, whether he knew that himself or not. Words were simply not necessary. God knows our hearts. And I see God roaming that street corner in Miami, searching for his lost lamb, my prodigal son. I will always love him. He was still so far away—from help and healing and asking for either—but I'm sure God was filled with compassion for him as he welcomed him to his true, final home. Michael's gain is my loss, but my heart is comforted knowing that he now realizes just how worthy he is.

It's painful for me that, to some people, Michael is just another statistic—one more name on a huge list of people who died a drug-related death during this terrible epidemic sweeping our country. To me, and to any of us who have lost someone to drug abuse, he was so much more than his addiction. I do not want his identity to be defined by it. Michael had the most compassionate heart. He was intelligent, and his cleverness shone through his hilarious antics. He loved to make others laugh. He adored his family. He was, and always will be, so well loved. I don't think he ever doubted that love, and knowing that he knew that does give me some peace, in the end.

My goal is to be in heaven with him someday, and while I long sometimes for it to be sooner rather than later, it must be in God's time and in God's way. Knowing Michael is in a place where he feels so much love makes it possible for me to get up and face each day. Michael always wanted to help us in some way. He's given us the ultimate gift by asking God to strengthen our hearts as we attempt to live in the world without him.

Pray for us, Michael. Pray for us.

I interviewed Jennifer by phone. It was apparent to me immediately that she loved her son very much. Loved? No, *loves*. Even though Michael is gone, she will always love him. She insisted that the connection she shared with him was unbreakable, even by death. Their bond cut both ways, though. Michael's behavior—and Jennifer's intense stress from watching heroin kill her son—affected her health:

"His addiction was tearing me up. I quit my teaching job when I found out he was using heroin. I just quit my job; I resigned. I couldn't focus on anything. Some people might think that we had an unhealthy attachment to each other, a little co-dependency, but I think that was because I was a young mother. Also, I was a single parent for so long. But yes. I see now the negative effect Michael's drug abuse had on me."

Jennifer got pregnant with Michael when she was a teenager. The sudden reality of young motherhood surprised her. It was a rude awakening. First, she didn't realize that she was pregnant. When she went to a clinic and discovered she was, her Catholic upbringing informed her decision to keep her child.

"When the doctor said to my mom, 'She does have options,' she just looked him dead in the eyes and said, 'An abortion is not one of them.'"

Jennifer said, "We talked about adoption too, and I actually did consider it, but it broke my parent's hearts that I would give up my baby to a friend or a relative. I wouldn't have been able to live with it—seeing him all the time and knowing he was my son."

Jennifer said that as soon as she gave birth, she had no doubt that keeping her baby was the right choice. She fell in love with Michael.

"Michael was a sweet baby. He was my little boy from the time he was old enough to have an attitude (he always kinda had one). But he was a good baby and very jolly and joyful—not colicky at all. Smart too."

Young motherhood was difficult, but she was devoted to providing a good life for her son. She married Michael's father, but his work kept him away. After their divorce, Michael's father moved back to his home state of Texas, making frequent visits to see his son very difficult. Jennifer had to carry the burden of parenting her son mostly as a single parent. She managed to finish high school while working long hours to provide diapers and food for her young family. She was sometimes painfully aware that she was missing out on the activities other young women her age were doing.

"I didn't go to football games and dances. I had a child to take care of! My focus was entirely on him. I remember lots of weekend babysitting jobs, not going to my prom, not going to football games, not spending time with my friends. My mom says she was very proud of me during that time when I took the reins."

Taking care of Michael became a central part of Jennifer's identity. At first, she could manage everything on her own, and she felt like she was on track to give him every opportunity and a good education. But the storm was ahead, and she couldn't stop the wind.

"Michael was very smart. I had him in preschool for ages four and five. When he was six, he started kindergarten. He went to the Catholic school that I went to. And he did very well. He liked school. He was good at school. There weren't really any problems until high school. Then things got really messy. Very scary."

It started after Michael was diagnosed with OCD. She said the meds helped him when he was on them, but that he refused to continue taking them when he got older. He didn't like the way they made him feel.

"He liked to be the center of attention. He was really great one-on-one, but if there were a lot of people around, he liked the attention to be focused on him a little bit too much. He started getting in trouble in class and for being the class goof. He got into a fight in middle school with another student and it earned him some status that he enjoyed."

From that time on, the pattern was set. Michael was out of control, and nothing Jennifer did seemed to make any difference. She couldn't influence him, stop him, or change him; if anything, her efforts seemed to make things worse. The love she felt for her son both benefited him and protected him from the full consequences of his drug abuse.

From what Jennifer shared with me, I discerned that Michael's drug use and behavior issues were different than mine had been. Michael didn't make much effort to hide his drug and alcohol abuse, whereas I had done everything I could to keep mine secret, hoping to protect my family from the monster I was becoming. I mention this difference because I believe Michael's brazen attitude and volatility accelerated his mother's decline in health, both physically and mentally.

"I had no control over him. He did not respect anything I ever said. I had to call the police on him sometimes, just to get him to mind me. I thought, *How did we go from a fairly normal kid to this?* And he said, *drugs.* He knew that the drugs had changed him, even then. And you know what? They changed me, too. I felt sick about him."

I wondered what she did to take care herself at this time. How did she get through it? What did she do to just get through the day?

She replied, "I had hope, and I just dug in my heels because that was what I was supposed to do. I thought, *I'm his mother and I'm the only parent he has to care for him.* I wasn't going to sit it out and watch him destroy himself—because I loved him."

I wondered if Jennifer genuinely believed that she could control her son's actions. She said, "Maybe I was a little overly controlling about it, but I just couldn't be idle and do nothing. I had to be proactive."

I've often thought about the "other side" of addiction. It wreaks horrific damage on the family and friends of the addict. My wife and I have discussed the same thing: what would we do if our children end up addicted? I can't imagine putting in one grain of sand less than the mountain of effort Jennifer had invested in Michael. I understand her drive to try to give him realistic solutions and opportunities to change his life. It's not hard to imagine her despair while she watched Michael's fatal trajectory, stuck on the path to inescapable disaster.

Jennifer wasn't the only one who saw the risk Michael was

placing himself in. She said, "The probation officer that had his first case looked at Michael and said, 'I don't understand you. You are not the typical kid we see in here. You're smart, you're good looking, you come from a very good family, and you are careening like a snowball down a steep hill right now—you're going straight down and gathering so much more as you go, and it's gonna be impossible to come back from it.'

"I remember him saying these things to Michael, and my mom and I sat there in the chairs on both sides of him crying, because we had no control. He was getting in trouble at school. He was getting in trouble with the law. He'd already been in juvenile five or six times by the time he quit high school."

Through all of her parenting drama, Jennifer also married two more times, which only added to the turmoil she was experiencing in her life. Thankfully, her current marriage has been a rock of stability. She's leaned on her husband while she copes with her son's death. She spoke through tears when she told me what happened the day she found out Michael was dead.

"I was just too distraught the day I found out he was gone. I couldn't even deal with it. I mean, I couldn't do *anything*. I was just too much of a mess. So Michael's dad made the arrangements for me. And the funeral director, he had Michael's body taken to a funeral home down in Florida. They had to get Michael and embalm him because he hadn't been embalmed. He'd been in a cooler for 12 days after the autopsy."

Through the entire, nightmarish story of her son's drug use, incarcerations, and multiple failed attempts to get and stay sober, Jennifer came to believe that shame, as well as heroin, killed Michael. The person he had become was so repulsive to himself, that he couldn't see any way back to a normal life. He craved forgiveness but wasn't able to reconcile what he'd done with the person he wanted to be. Like his addiction, his shame had him trapped.

"He told me that while he lived at Hope House, when the

pastors would come and talk to him, he would ask them questions about whether God could forgive him for the things he'd done. But he told Ms. Whitney, the center's administrator, 'You don't understand what I've done. If you knew, you would never say that God forgives me. God can't forgive me. I'm at the point of no return.'"

For all the shame Michael felt, Jennifer never stopped telling him that she loved him unconditionally. She also never stopped praying for him, hoping that God would heal his addiction. Her faith had always been important to her. Through this trial, it became the one solace she could turn to. Near the end of our conversation, she shared a quote by Dostoyevsky she received from her therapist:

> Love a man even in his sin, for that love is a likeness of the divine love, and is the summit of love on earth. Love all God's creation, both the whole and every grain of sand. Love every leaf, every ray of light. Love the animals, love the plants, love each separate thing. If thou love each thing, thou wilt perceive the mystery of God in all; and when once thou perceive this, thou wilt thenceforward grow every day to a fuller understanding of it: until thou come at last to love the whole world with a love that will then be all-embracing and universal.[37]

Why these lines? What had made such a strong impression on her? Jennifer said, "My grief therapist sent it to me, because it feels like my biggest struggle is that I love my son, and that love has not stopped and that love *will not* stop growing. It's

---

[37] Dostoevski, Fyodor. 1970. *The Brothers Karamazov*. New York: Random House. 355.

just that I have nowhere for it to go! I mean, Michael's gone now. Even though I know he's in heaven—I believe that he's in heaven, that God is compassionate and merciful—I don't believe that Michael ever had to open his mouth and say, *I'm sorry.*

"I believe God knows our hearts and knows how sorry he really he was and how terrible he felt for the things that he'd done. I feel like I loved him deeply throughout all of this. Did I get angry with him? Yes. But I never failed to tell him that I loved him, and my love still grows for him even though he's not here." She started to cry.

"But the love has nowhere to go! I mean, it's a big struggle for me right now, because for 13 years I've tried to be the person that saved him, helped him. And I'm learning now: that wasn't my job."

I asked her where she thought all that love would take her, and what she would do with it.

She said, "Well, I don't know. I hope to do something. I pray about this every day, that God will lead me in the direction that will honor God, and that will honor Michael's struggle in some way."

It wasn't a neat and clean plan of action. Her pain was still so present, so close to the surface. Instead of reaching for a support network, like Al-Anon, Jennifer had worn herself raw with anxiety. She was emotionally and physically exhausted. The phone seemed to vibrate against my ear as she took a long breath.

"Could I tell Michael's story? Could I maybe spread awareness? Yeah, I could do all of those things," she said. "I want to tell you something: if somebody asked me what Michael's greatest character gift was, I would say it was his empathy. Michael was the most compassionate person I knew. He would notice an older person eating alone in a restaurant when he was seven or eight years old. He shared his food with the older jailbird who didn't have somebody to put money on his books and get snacks in the commissary. He was the one that would reach out to the underdog."

It didn't surprise me. Jennifer was extremely kind and compassionate; it wasn't hard to believe that Michael had learned those spiritual tools at home. When I suggested it, Jennifer laughed.

"I think that's what my mother would say. I think about the idea of sharing my pain with other parents because I do feel compassion for others who are now struggling with their addicted children. I know how they feel. I know what they're going through, and I know what their fears are. If I could channel my love for Michael to them, I think that might make a difference. Michael always said, 'If I ever make it through this fire, I will be able to help somebody.' I even put that quote in his obituary. And maybe that's the case for me, too."

Listening to Jennifer's story gave me goosebumps. Part of it was the way she talked so courageously about her struggles with her son and the pain of losing him. But I also witnessed her discovery of her deep power, and the inspiration that might help her keep going. Her transformation was both wonderful and inspiring. Whether she knew it or not, I believe she was identifying the spiritual asset that served as the foundation for her resilience: *her love.* She recognized that she still loves her son, but that "it has nowhere to go." She realized that other people are hurting, too; she hoped to honor Michael's life by directing her love for him into channels to ease others' pain. In a way, Michael's wish to make it "out of the fire" has been realized. His desire to make a difference will bear fruit through his mother's love directed to help others.

I had faith that she could do it—and proof too. As she

healed and contended with her grief, Jennifer's compassion grew to extend to many other people, even those who may have contributed in some way to her son's addiction. One woman, who contacted Jennifer after Michael's death, was there the first time Michael picked up a needle.

Jennifer said, "She has a lot of guilt. She says she tried to talk him out of it. She contacted me right after she found out Michael died. She was horrified by his death and told me she felt like it was her fault. *Wait. What?* I thought. She told me she wanted to come to his calling and his funeral. She wanted to pay her respects. At first I thought, *No! You are not welcome here.* But then I prayed, and I thought, *Jennifer, is it really her fault?* If Michael was going to be doing heroin, he would have found himself in the presence of it and done it. Today she's been clean and sober for four years; she's married and has a child and she totally changed her life. I saw her at the funeral and we hugged and cried together."

Resilience and Love

I'll start with a disclaimer. I'm initially always hesitant to use Biblical quotes in my writing. I suppose it's because I don't want to turn off a reader who claims a different authority than I do. I also loathe the thought that you might see the quotation and instantly assume, *Oh, he's one of those Bible-quotin' types.* All I can do is to be as honest as I can with the tradition as it has been passed down to me while staying open to the truth of other spiritual traditions.

As a progressive Christian, I believe the Christian scriptures have a lot to say about love. I'm not talking about the syrupy, Hallmark card type of love, either. The love I'm referring to is much deeper, much more self-giving. It's divine, which means that it defies human expectations and definitions. This love is perfect, all-encompassing, and beyond anything our imaginations could conjure up. To even get close to describing it, I realized I needed to look to the wisdom of scripture, both from my own tradition, and others. These rich traditions help lay a foundation for a definition of love. They also concisely define what love is not.

When I was a pastor serving in western North Dakota, I presided at lots of weddings. Easily over half of them featured a scripture reading from 1 Corinthians 13. If you've been to a Christian wedding, you've probably heard this one:

> If I speak in the tongues of mortals and of angels, but do not have love, I am a noisy gong or a clanging cymbal. And if I have prophetic powers, and understand all mysteries and all knowledge, and if I have all faith, so as to remove mountains, but do not have love, I am nothing. If I give away all my possessions, and if I hand over my body so that I may boast, but do not have love, I gain nothing. Love is patient; love is kind; love is not envious or boastful or arrogant or rude. It does not insist on its own way; it is not irritable or resentful; it does not rejoice in wrongdoing, but rejoices in the truth. It bears all things, believes all things, hopes all things, endures all things. Love never ends.[38]

It makes sense that couples often single out this text for their weddings—after all, what human bond has more potential for conflict than marriage? Any couple would need love to survive. However, Apostle Paul wrote the First Epistle to the Corinthians in the belief that love would unite an agitated community

---

[38] 1 Cor. 13:1-8a NRSV

distraught with disagreement and bickering. I believe Paul explicitly calls attention to love, "the greatest of these," because he knew that of all the virtues, love alone reflects the self-giving compassion of the Infinite One in every respect.

Take another view of the New Testament from the first Letter of John: "Beloved, let us love one another, because love is from God; everyone who loves is born of God and knows God. Whoever does not love does not know God, for God is love."[39] From the same chapter: "There is no fear in love, but perfect love casts out fear; for fear has to do with punishment, and whoever fears has not reached perfection in love."[40] The writer first describes that love dwells at the heart of God, and second clarifies how love casts out fear. Interestingly, the writer defines fear as the antithesis of love, not hate or anger, two negative human expressions that perhaps come more easily to mind as the opposite of love.

Other spiritual traditions are teeming with the concept of love.

- Islam: "The reward of love is nothing but love it-self."[41]

- Hinduism: "The one who loves all intensely begins perceiving in all living beings a part of himself. He becomes a lover of all, a part and parcel of the Universal Joy. He flows with the stream of happiness, and is enriched by each soul."[42]

- Judaism: "Hatred stirs up strife, but love covers all

---

[39] 1 John 4:7-8 NRSV
[40] 1 John 4:18 NRSV
[41] Al Quran 55:61
[42] Yajur-Veda, Kanda III.

offenses."[43]

- Buddhism: "Love the whole world as a mother loves her only child."[44]

To be sure, love serves as a common theme throughout many of the world's great religions.

Love also plays an important role to describe the best of human virtues from a secular point of view. Here's another one of my favorites from Viktor Frankl in *Man's Search for Meaning*:

> [F]or the first time in my life I saw the truth as it is set into song by so many poets, proclaimed as the final wisdom by so many thinkers. The truth— that love is the ultimate and the highest goal to which [a person] can aspire. Then I grasped the meaning of the greatest secret that human poetry and human thought and belief have to impart: The salvation of [human beings] is through love and in love. I understood how a [person] who has nothing left in this world still may know bliss, be it only for a brief moment, in the contemplation of [the] beloved. In a position of utter desolation, when [a person] cannot express [themselves] in positive action, when [their] only achievement may consist in enduring sufferings in the right way—an honorable way— in such a position [a person] can, through loving contemplation of the image [they] carry of [the] beloved, achieve fulfillment. For the first time in my life I was able to understand the meaning of the words, "The

---

[43] Prov. 10:12 The Hebrew Bible.
[44] Attr. Gautama Buddha.

angels are lost in perpetual contemplation of an
infinite glory."[45]

Frankl describes a love that can overcome personal tragedy and
trauma, including even the horrors of a Nazi concentration
camp.

Clearly, love is a good thing. But how does love contribute
as a spiritual asset to a person's resilience? In what way does
love become a virtue or wellspring from which a person may
draw strength *to see more clearly, love more deeply, and act more
courageously* in the face of trauma or hardship? Most importantly, how does Jennifer's love for her son serve as her own
spiritual asset for resilience? I believe the way to get at these
questions is to first identify what love speaks against and what
loves speaks for.

If fear is the opposite of love then love stands over against
fear. Carl Gustav Jung, the Swiss psychiatrist and psychologist,
speculated that human beings have certain traits that we hide
from others. From the time we were children, we gradually
came to understand that this behavior was necessary if we
wanted to be accepted. Our need for acceptance (and, I'd add
the evolutionary value of fear to a person's survival as a social
creature) compels us to create a self to fit in, not lose face, and
develop what Sigmund Freud called "the ideal ego."

The difficulty with developing a strong ego we wear like an
unsightly wart is that we cannot learn to love ourselves, or by
extension, others, based on fear. To love yourself unconditionally means to accept yourself, recognize yourself, or even be
rejected by others, *without fear*. Loving yourself doesn't mean
becoming a self-absorbed narcissist; that's different. Truly loving
yourself instead indicates that you are willing to allow yourself

---

[45] Frankl, Viktor Emil. 1992. *Man's Search for Meaning.* Boston: Beacon
Press. 48,49.

to simply be, "warts and all." By truly loving yourself in this way, it allows you to love others. Because you allow yourself to simply be, you can consent to others' existence as they choose to be. A full, perfect love even allows the possibility of losing your own life for the sake of another. Full love drives out the fear of punishment or lack of acceptance, for you and for others.

In Jennifer's case, it meant that she loved Michael enough to allow him to make his own choices, even though she knew those choices might spell disaster. I'm not saying that she simply acquiesced to her son's will. She did the opposite, in fact—she set clear boundaries and provided guidance. She did this imperfectly, but after all, she is human. Very few achieve a perfect love in this life. Jennifer was not afraid to speak the truth in love. She didn't act out of fear to control Michael, which is the other aspect love speaks against: possessiveness and control.

I believe God designed creation for freedom. We were not meant to be enslaved by each other; we're meant to love each other freely instead. It's similar to the concept of the marriage relationship: each partner allows the other to simply be. Henry Cloud wrote in *Boundaries in Marriage*, "Marriage is not slavery. It is based on a love relationship deeply rooted in freedom. Each partner is free from the other and therefore free to love the other. Where there is control, or perception of control, there is not love. Love only exists where there is freedom."[46] The same can be said about any relationship founded in love.

Jennifer admitted that she struggled with the need to do something to help her son, or in her words, "be proactive." Addiction is insidious: it compels family, friends, and loved ones into action. We don't want to lose the person we care about! Still, loving freely—without the need for control or the fear of punishment—means that we tell the truth when it

---

[46] Dr. Henry Cloud & Dr. Townsend John. 1999. *Boundaries in Marriage*. Grand Rapids, MI: Zondervan.

needs telling and that we make the best decisions we possibly can without adversely affecting our own serenity. Jennifer loved as best she could; perhaps that sometimes blurred into the realm of codependency. However, it's hopeful to hear in her own words, "For thirteen years I've tried to be the person that saved him, helped him. And I'm learning now, that wasn't my job." Jennifer is committed to growing in her understanding of love. Whether our inspiration comes from a tragic loss or a momentary epiphany, this path is open to us, as well. When we're coping with addiction and its devastating effects, it may be the only path.

So, what does love speak *for*? How does love become a spiritual asset to strengthen a person's resiliency to trauma? Harry Frankfurt, in his groundbreaking work on the topic of love, defines love as "a disinterested concern for the existence of what is loved, and for what is good for it."[47] The word *disinterested* is at first misleading. However, what the author is implying is that true love doesn't have an ulterior motive. "The lover desires that [the] beloved flourish and not be harmed; and he [or she] does not desire this just for the sake of promoting some other goal."[48]

Love speaks for the wellbeing of all humanity. Love builds bridges and seeks connection. Love creates relationships and celebrates life-giving differences. Without this self-giving, self-loving love, our speech is "… like a noisy gong, or clanging cymbal." With it, it "rejoices in the truth. It bears all things, believes all things, hopes all things, endures all things." Love speaks not only for what it means to be authentically human, but also defines the very character of the divine.

Perhaps nowhere else is this loving relationship witnessed

---

[47] Frankfurt, H.G. 2004. *The Reasons of Love*. Princeton: Princeton University Press. 42.
[48] Ibid.

more than in the relationship between a mother and her child. Jennifer immediately fell in love with Michael, simply because he was her baby. As a man, I envy women in some ways—they alone carry a child, feel his first movements in the womb, and bond with him in a deep intimacy that seems to exclude the rest of the world. For certain, fathers also love their children, but we do not enjoy (or struggle with!) the tenderness and intimacy a mother has for her child.

Jennifer never gave up loving Michael. Through every disappointment, arrest, and new revelation that he had failed again, she never ceased loving her son. His shame separated him from God, but it couldn't keep him away from Jennifer. Her love even extended beyond the barrier of death. In her own words: "I feel like I loved Michael deeply throughout all of this. Did I get angry with him? Yes. But I never failed to tell him that I loved him, and my love still grows for him even though he's not here. But the love ... it has nowhere to go!"

Jennifer is in the beginning stages of grief. However, her discovery that she can make a difference for others, that she still has a purpose, is significant. Her life has meaning, which creates a direction for her love she feels for her son. In her words, "If I could channel my love for Michael to them, I think that might make a difference."

She also sees that Michael's compassionate goal to "get through the fire" and "make a difference" still can be realized, only in a different way than either of them might have wanted. It's this *redirected* love that gives Jennifer the hope for a new day. Love provides resilience, bit by bit. Building resilience, just like opening up to love, is like building muscle: it pushes us beyond our personal comfort zones so that we grow and become stronger, more flexible. Love challenges us to look beyond ourselves, calls us to embrace even the things and people that cause us the most pain, and soothes us while we accept excruciating loss with grace. Love points us to the ultimate meaning of life: to engage with the world on God's terms, with love, and without fear.

In one last bit of correspondence, Jennifer offered another insight about her situation that I found both hopeful and touching:

"Since life was such a struggle with Michael for so long, I am beginning to feel the possibility of our love for each other being stronger in death than in life. Why? Because everything negative and dark has been erased. It's gone. Now, all that's left is love. And it continues to grow. Is it possible that I could have a stronger, deeper, more meaningful and powerful relationship with my son in death than I did in life? Time will tell."

Afterword

Writing this book was hard work; it was probably the most difficult and long-suffering task I have ever undertaken. When I began molding the form of it nearly three-and-a-half years ago, even the title and the topic were different. Originally, I wanted to write a work outlining each of the Twelve Steps through other people's stories. Every chapter would highlight another Step in the recovery process. Its title would have been *Your Story is Not Yet Finished.* Through every person's story and each new Step, I would discover for myself (and pass along to the reader) the process of personal transformation, specifically how it related to recovery from addiction to drugs and alcohol.

However, I began to recognize that I wasn't interested only in the process of personal change from the viewpoint of addiction-recovery. Simultaneously, my online blog *Transformation is Real* began to shift its focus as well, highlighting and categorizing personal transformation from the rich mosaic of changes that people make in their lives. Despite the differences between each person's story, one common thread revealed itself. From stories of survival after a sexual assault, to the tales behind a tattoo someone chose to mark a personal change, to addiction-recovery fiction and micro-poetry, even stories sharing how service to others leads to meaning and purpose—the one, shared trait to rise from the ashes of stress or trauma to make

190

lasting change was resilience.

I am not a trained psychologist. My educational background is in theology. Since my vocational change over six years ago, I've become a freelance writer and award-winning author. Fiction was my first love, and to this day I find sitting down at my laptop to knead the Promethean molding-clay in my head into a story far more engaging (and fun) than building a systematic argument that reads like a Pauline diatribe. But I'm not alone in that regard. It stands to reason that the stories from a person's faith tradition tend to be more memorable than reasoned arguments. Human beings, after all, are story creatures; stories capture our attention easier than reasoned truths.

However, the main focus for this book still stared back at me: how should I make the case that spiritual assets such as honesty, gratitude, acceptance, hope, faith, forgiveness, or love positively influence a person's capacity to find their innate resilience? I can rest easy knowing that this compilation of others' stories of resilience and how they relate has accomplished this task for two reasons.

First, virtues or spiritual assets are not quantifiable. I don't have X amount of gratitude while you have Y, and where George has Z amount of hope, Colin only has Z minus three. Spirituality doesn't work that way. Spirituality and each spiritual asset are nebulous and only understandable within the narrative of each person's story. That is to say that they are subjective. We can say what each spiritual asset is not, however. We know that Hitler and Gandhi had different expressions of what love is or should be, for example.

Second, resilience isn't quantifiable either. By its own definition, resilience is situationally and shock-specific. One common formula I found in all my reading is that resilience is *of whom, to what*. Although some have attempted to place normative values (such as the "costs" an individual or household has gone through to live through a particular trauma[49]) to specific responses for any single stressful or traumatic situation, the fact of the matter is that resilience is subjective. Like spirituality, however, we can say that one person exhibited resilience while another did not.

Is there really a correlation between spirituality (and specific spiritual assets) and resilience? From my viewpoint, yes. The literature already published seems to corroborate this as well.[50] From the direction I've taken in this book, each narrative from me, Cathy, Hunter, Raja, Kitty, Rick, and Jennifer suggest that finding meaning through each spiritual asset and integrating it into the larger framework of a life not only makes a difference in the response, but also aids a person to look beyond the dreck that life inevitably throws our way.

Resilience is both about perspective but also the response. Spirituality and the specific spiritual assets that build a larger framework of a belief system are tools to assist a person within the human condition. Ultimately, these tools help us to overcome whatever shock comes our way.

Rather than continuing to stir this stew of a systematic

[49] For further reading, see: Béné, Christophe. 2013. *Towards a Quantifiable Measure of Resilience*. England: Institute of Development Studies.
http://www.ids.ac.uk/publication/towards-a-quantifiable-measure-of-resilience
[50] See: Peres, Julio F. P., Alexander Moreira-Almeida, Antonia Gladys Nasello, and Harold G. Koenig. 2006. *Spirituality and Resilience in Trauma Victims*. Blanton-Peale Institute.
http://www.julioperes.com.br/upload/files/SpiritualityResilience2007.pdf

argument I've seemed to embroil myself in, let me conclude with a story. Stories, after all, speak to unquantifiable truths much better than dissecting them to discover their constituent parts or their relationships to each other. The story comes from a tiny book I read back in my undergraduate days at Concordia College in Moorhead, Minnesota. The book is a mix of both prose and poetry and continues to stir in my thoughts to this day.

In his book *Invisible Cities*, the author Italo Calvino masterfully weaves the tale of a series of discussions between the Mongol emperor Kublai Kahn and the Venetian explorer Marco Polo. Kublai Kahn correctly discerns the coming fall of his empire and intimates to his guest Marco Polo of his frustration. Marco Polo regales his host with stories of cities, using what knowledge he had gained in his travels to show that, "Cities, like dreams, are made of desires and fears. Even if the thread of their discourse is secret, their rules are absurd, their perspectives deceitful, and everything conceals something else."[51] Marco Polo seeks to show that human beings, like cities, are more than the sum of their parts or the conquests they have overcome.

One passage from this book I've never forgotten is a perfect allegory to show how spiritual assets build resilience. It illustrates that the whole of a person's response to trauma or stress is more than the assets that build it, but without them, a positive response cannot exist. In Calvino's book, Marco Polo is describing a bridge, stone by stone. After which comes the following discourse between the two men:

"But which is the stone that supports the bridge?" Kublai Khan asks.

"The bridge is not supported by one stone or

---

[51] Calvino, Italo. 2013. *Invisible Cities*. Mariner Books. 44.

another," Marco answers, "but by the line of the arch that they form."

Kublai Khan remains silent, reflecting. Then he adds: "Why do you speak to me of the stones? It is only the arch that matters to me."

Polo answers: "Without stones, there is no arch."[52]

Without the stones of spiritual assets a person may employ, the bridge to resilience (the arch) is unattainable. How each stone fits into the arch may not be quantifiable or even discernable from a distance, but we know that each bit contributes to the whole just as much as atoms make molecules and molecules form physical matter. It is my hope that, through this book, that others will discover spiritual assets—the inheritance any human being has—to overcome the losses, stresses, traumas, and difficulty life invariably brings.

Follow Up

As I began writing this book, many of the people's lives have continued. Here is a brief follow up what has taken place since I began writing:

Cathy's attacker has since been sentenced to one term of life in prison in Mississippi and is awaiting a sentencing for his second offense of kidnapping. Cathy has since moved back to Minnesota where she has been attending school. Her dream is to create an outreach for women who find themselves in similar situations of abuse. She plans to speak publicly and share her

---

[52] Ibid. 82.

story of survival, and how her gratitude for her life keeps her pointed the right direction.

Hunter is currently between military deployments and lives with his family stateside. I correspond with him occasionally and continue to be entertained by his unique sense of humor and perspective on life.

Raja has since attained the reunification with his family and currently lives in Berlin, Germany after his stay in Greece. With the ongoing conflict in Syria, an end seems nowhere in sight. Also furthering the difficulties for refugee families is the current wave of nationalism and anti-immigrant hysteria that seems to have engulfed the world. I remain hopefully optimistic that rationality and compassion will win out in the end and will allow Raja eventually to return to his homeland.

Kitty lives in her home in northern Minnesota that she and her husband had built. She keeps herself busy through volunteering in her church and community. She has since pieced together more of the puzzle of her sister's murder and the relationships she has with her family. She plans to share how her faith continues to inform not only her ability to thrive, but also how it provides meaning and purpose to her life.

Rick is an ordained Lutheran minister in the ELCA and lives in Washington State with his second wife. He frequently speaks on the power of forgiveness and how it served as a meaningful foundation for his ministry, as well as the defining moment of his life.

Jennifer's story of the loss of her son to addiction continues to be a challenging difficulty. She continues to be an active participant in online social media forums. Jennifer has recently resumed teaching, and her story has yet to unfold to reveal how her love for her son remains her greatest asset to help others overcome losses from the epidemic of opioid addiction that has swept this country.

I continue to keep up my blog *Transformation is Real* and

speak on the transformative power of life-change. Through this book, I hope to teach others that spirituality does not have to be a scary, excluding, or arcane process, but instead that a spiritual life is a never-ending quest to become a more authentic, whole human being.

CPSIA information can be obtained
at www.ICGtesting.com
Printed in the USA
LVOW11s0836071017
551581LV00002B/279/P